The Revd Dr Trystan Owain Hughes
Cardiff University. He attained an M
from Oxford University and a PhD in twentieth-century church
history from Bangor University, Wales. He is a regular con-
tributor to BBC Radio 2's *Pause for Thought* and BBC Radio
4's *Prayer for the Day*. He is the author of the widely acclaimed
Finding Hope and Meaning in Suffering (SPCK, 2010), which
was serialized in the *Church Times* and was the Archbishop of
Wales's 2011 Lent Book. He lectures in theology at Cardiff
University and has spoken at retreats, quiet days and conferences worldwide, including in Germany, Australia, India and
the USA.

THE COMPASSION QUEST

Trystan Owain Hughes

First published in Great Britain in 2013

Society for Promoting Christian Knowledge
36 Causton Street
London SW1P 4ST
www.spckpublishing.co.uk

British Library Cataloguing-in-Publication Data
A catalogue record for this book is available from the British Library

ISBN 978–0–281–06825–8
eBook ISBN 978–0–281–06826–5

Typeset by Graphicraft Limited, Hong Kong
First printed in Great Britain by Ashford Colour Press
Subsequently digitally printed in Great Britain

Produced on paper from sustainable forests

Contents

To Sandra, Lukas and Lena

Piglet: 'How do you spell "love"?'
Pooh: 'You don't spell it. You feel it.'
A. A. Milne

Acknowledgements

Diolch o'r galon ('thanks from the heart') to all who have assisted and supported me during the writing of this book. Thank you especially to all who have shown me the meaning of compassion in every stage of my life journey – in Penmaenmawr, Bangor, Carmarthen, Oxford, Llantwit Major, Whitchurch, and at Cardiff University.

More specifically I would like to thank:

All those who gave advice on parts of the book (whether they realized it or not!) – Perry Buck, Ros Hughes, Katja Neubauer, Kath Lawley, Nat Garrett, Emil Evans, Charlotte Trombin, Anna Dakin, Naomi Hodge, Delyth Liddell, James and Kath Fathers, Peter Lacey and Chris Burr.

Archbishop Barry Morgan, Bishop David Wilbourne, and others in the Diocese of Llandaff for supporting my ministry with love and understanding.

Gwydion Thomas for permission to use an extract from R. S. Thomas' poem 'Cynddylan on a Tractor'.

All at SPCK for believing that others would want to read the book, and especially to Alison Barr for her support and astute suggestions.

My mum (Ros), dad (Berw), and my brothers (Marc, Dyfan and Gwynan) and sister (Angharad) with all their wonderful families, for their continual support and love.

Since my last book, *Finding Hope and Meaning in Suffering*, was published, God has blessed my life in ways I never imagined possible. Most of all, I met and married my beautiful wife Sandra and became a dad to two delightful children, Lukas and Lena, who have provided inspiration, love, and so much fun and laughter throughout the process of writing. Sandra herself is no stranger to both compassion and suffering, having been widowed at a young age, and so she has been able to give countless insightful suggestions on the text and has enthusiastically and tirelessly read drafts of the book. She has also been a rock of support and love. I owe her so much. I never realized that three people could bring me so much happiness and fulfilment. I thank God daily for bringing them into my life.

Prologue: finding our purpose

Life is beautiful and worth living and meaningful. Despite everything.

Etty Hillesum, 12 months before her death in Auschwitz

May God bless you with enough foolishness to believe that you can make a difference in this world, so that you can do what others claim cannot be done.

Franciscan Benediction

In Brian Selznick's novel *The Invention of Hugo Cabret*, later adapted into the hit movie *Hugo* by director Martin Scorsese, the eponymous 12-year-old hero discusses the meaning of life with his friend Isabelle. Pondering the clockwork machines that he had painstakingly restored, he comes to the conclusion that all machines are created by humans for specific reasons. 'They are built to make you laugh, like the mouse here,' he says, as the couple watch a wind-up mouse skittle across the table, 'or to tell the time, like clocks, or to fill you with wonder.' He then admits that broken machines bring sadness to his heart, as they are not fulfilling the purpose of their creation. 'Maybe it's the same with people,' he concludes, 'if you lose your purpose, it's like you're broken.'

The secular world has developed a deep-seated fear of the Christian concept of 'sin', holding that it induces an unhealthy amount of individual guilt. Such criticism is not without validity, and, as a result, even my colleagues in the Church are rarely brave enough to tackle the subject directly in their sermons or teaching. The musings of Hugo Cabret, however, hint at something of what the Bible is referring to when it asserts that we are living in a 'sinful' world. After all, in many ways we are alienated from our intended purpose. We live in a 'broken' world, which has lost its reason for being. But that, of course, is not the end of the story. Just as the orphan boy Hugo is brought hope and purpose through his young friend Isabelle, who is the first person for many years to show him compassion and love, it is in the quest for those very qualities, compassion and love, that all of us can find the reason for our existence.

In my last book, *Finding Hope and Meaning in Suffering*, I intended to show that hope and meaning can be found even in the midst of great adversity. Our greatest gift in facing our suffering is the present moment, which is where God resides. It is in the here and now that we are able to connect with the world in all its wonder and thus touch the divine. The transcendent dwells in life's details. He is present in the people we meet, in the beauty of nature, in the bliss of silence, in the comfort of our memories, and in the joy of laughter. In fact, we can find God in most of our seemingly ordinary and everyday experiences. 'Shut your mouth; open your eyes and ears,' writes C. S. Lewis; 'take in what there is and give no thought to what might have been there or what is somewhere else.'

This book is also about the present moment, but the emphasis is now widened. Not only do we appreciate that the here and now can bring meaning to our own lives, but we recognize, too, that our own present moments can bring light to the lives of others. We live in a society where achievements, wealth and success are, by and large, valued higher than altruistic actions. Responsibility for those suffering, for those in the throes of injustice and for environmental concerns is, therefore, sometimes overlooked, as individual endeavour and greed is, often unconsciously, championed. There are signs, however, that a new paradigm is emerging, where we are beginning to recognize that the cult of celebrity, the obsession of lust and the glorifying of power are false gods. In the words of T. S. Eliot, increasingly many of us no longer feel at ease 'in the old dispensation'. By using the present moment to be present to each other, we can choose another way of living, as we stand alongside others who suffer and share willingly in their vulnerability, weakness and uncertainty. It is, after all, when we attune ourselves to love's frequency that the quest for meaning, purpose and strength can be fulfilled.

This fact became particularly clear to me during two periods of my life. First, a number of years ago, I underwent a period of intense pain and suffering. During that time I was diagnosed with a degenerative back condition and underwent spinal surgery. For almost a year I was restricted to lying down at home – alone, unable to work, and limited to only short, pain-filled walks each day. One morning, I struggled downstairs to answer my front door. On the step stood a 24-year-old man, whom I had only met once before in passing, at a funeral at which I had officiated. The young man announced that he had heard of my back injury and knew that I lived alone, so he was wondering whether he could help with any household chores. For the next six months, James came over to my house regularly, at least once a week, and would do my washing up, empty my bins, and do my grocery shopping for me. Outwardly, his altruism offered no real gain for this popular and trendy young man, who was training to be a lawyer. His assistance was not born out of a sense of duty and it was not done for any payment. Furthermore, he was not a churchgoer, so there was no outward religious incentive. Yet his visits did not simply bring help to me at a time of helplessness. I recall him later disclosing to me that he had no real idea what had inspired him to offer support, but in his little acts of compassionate kindness he had found a meaning that was beyond anything he was experiencing in his life of partying and studying.

The other event that helped bring me to a realization that meaning and purpose are forged through compassion occurred in my first year of ministering in a church in Cardiff. A member of my congregation asked me to visit her work colleague's father, who had been diagnosed with a brain tumour. Over the next three months I visited Ray's bedside regularly, and my time with him had a profound effect on me. I would always walk in to a barrage of abuse about my beloved Swansea City football team, as he was a fan of our greatest rivals, Cardiff City! The rest of the time with him was spent chatting, debating, laughing and crying. During the last two weeks of his life I visited him daily, often simply to hold his hand and then to drink coffee with his struggling family. At his funeral, his grieving wife told me that my presence at his bedside had brought much comfort and hope to this non-church-attender. Yet, in my mind, the purpose and meaning that had been engendered had been mutual in a way I would never have imagined, and I was walking away from our short association having been deeply affected.

Compassion in the present moment can certainly bring a purpose and reason to a world that seems to struggle with locating significance. *Finding Hope and Meaning in Suffering*'s emphasis on the importance of discovering individual inner meaning rooted itself firmly in the biblical tradition, but it also laid its foundations in the Christian contemplative tradition. It particularly advocated two concepts that have been at the heart of contemplative Christianity down the centuries. The concept of *awareness* leads us to connect with the present moment in such a way that we can recognize it for what it truly is – a loving experience of the kingdom of God. Alongside this is the concept of *acceptance*, which, rather than being passive submission to hardships, is a transformative embracing of the reality of situations. There is, however, a third area that has underpinned much of the contemplative tradition down the ages, a concept that I left unexplored in my earlier book. This is *interconnectedness*, which values the mutual relationship between our inner being and the outside world.

The interconnectedness of God's creation was briefly touched upon in the chapters on 'Nature' and 'Helping others' in *Finding Hope and Meaning in Suffering*, but the concept was generally sidelined, as the book was fundamentally inward-looking and centred on individual spirituality. This book attempts to redress the balance. Our spiritual journey, after all, must do more than merely assist us as individuals, lest it descend into a mere tool for self-help and positive thinking. Down the years, Christian spirituality has tended towards issues of our inner life, and, in recent years at least, even worship has become increasingly insular and me-focused. As a consequence, for many years Christians have been led away from a holistic reading of the Bible and theology. A truly biblical understanding of our spiritual life, however, relates to our whole existence, not least to our relationships with God, with each other, and with the rest of the created world. The US civil rights movement of the 1960s, for example, recognized the importance of such a holistic vision of spirituality. God was working through both personal and social dimensions of the civil rights leaders, and their personal relationships with God were inseparable from their tireless work for justice and reconciliation. Both dimensions complemented each other. Thus our personal spiritual lives are very much related to the social dimension of our lives. To separate our inward and outward journeys is to set up a false dichotomy. The two are inseparable parts of one experience, and we should never make rivals of soul and body, sacred and secular, spirit and flesh, or Church and world.

As such, any theological reflection on spirituality cannot ignore how imperative it is for us to give physicality to our inner lives. The words in any book on theology are as worthless as the paper they are written on if they remain merely black ink on the page. Our theology cannot remain incarcerated in academic textbooks or caged up in religious buildings. Karl Marx observed that philosophers tend to interpret the world, when they should be trying to change the world. Likewise, theology should not be about words, however useful they are for sharing ideas. Clarence Jordan warned of the consequences of incarcerating the Word (the *logos*) in intellectual pursuits:

The Word became a sermon and was later expanded into a book and the book sold well and inspired other books until of the making of books there was no end. And the Word died in darkness and was buried in the theological library.

For the Word to thrive, theology should be not only about observing, but also about acting. In John's Gospel, Jesus' very first words are to a group of John the Baptist's disciples (John 1.35–39). 'What do you want?' he asks. The disciples respond, rather strangely, with another question: 'where are you staying?' Jesus answers with a simple invitation: 'Come and see.' Theology is about exactly that – looking and seeing, and then responding in action to what we have seen.

It was with this logic in mind that Hans Urs von Balthasar claimed that true theologians do not simply ruminate on doctrines, but rather they observe the life of Christ and then live out what they have seen. This is the only way, according to him, to true 'sainthood'. The fact that so many Christians before us have not lived out the theology they espoused is a stark warning to us all. German guards at Auschwitz would sometimes wear belt buckles on their uniforms that proclaimed 'God with us', then sit at home in the evenings listening to Bach's spiritual classics. Our theology and spirituality must never be something that is compartmentalized, kept away from our everyday routines. Rather, it must be integral to every part of our lives. As Etty Hillesum put it: 'I keep talking about God the whole day long, and it is high time that I lived accordingly.'

1

Faith and the universe

———•◆•———

Just as a circle embraces all that is within it, so does the
Godhead embrace all. No one has the power to divide this
circle.

> *Hildegard of Bingen, twelfth-century contemplative*

Look deep into nature, and then you will understand
everything better.

> *Albert Einstein*

In Alice Walker's Pulitzer Prize-winning novel *The Color Purple*,
the main protagonist, Celie, a poor, uneducated black girl
living in the Deep South of the United States in the 1930s,
describes to a friend the God to which she was introduced at
a very young age. 'He big and old and tall and greybearded and
white,' she explains, 'you wear white robes and go barefooted.'
This God was a distant, authoritarian figure, who had been
used for centuries to justify the power that whites held over
blacks and that men held over women. Celie admits that it was,
therefore, easy for her to discard her outdated white, male deity.
'When I found out, I thought God was white, and a man, I lost
interest,' she confesses. This, however, was only the beginning
of Celie's faith journey, and the novel describes her eventually
laying aside her negative concept of God and moving towards
a radically different, incarnational portrayal of the divine.

While very few Christians today would hold to a God who
could be described as 'white' and a 'man', a theologically traditional view of God is still in ascendance. Yet in recent years the
traditional image of God has found itself under vitriolic attack.

Writers such as Richard Dawkins and the late Christopher Hitchens have certainly influenced the thoughts and beliefs of their readers, but more than this they reflect and affirm the already deeply held hostility of an increasingly atheistic society towards faith. Speaking about 'God' is regarded as being as nonsensical as speaking about Father Christmas or the tooth fairy. 'Fairies don't exist, because we don't see them. If we don't see things, they don't exist,' explained my five-year-old daughter. Dawkins' analogy of faith being akin to believing in a Flying Spaghetti Monster runs along a similar line of argument – believing in a God that we can't 'see', 'touch' or 'hear' is as ridiculous as believing in a fantastical creature. Dawkins' image has particularly been taken into the hearts of atheist and agnostic internet bloggers, one of whom famously adapted an image of Michelangelo's ceiling at the Sistine Chapel by replacing the Almighty with the Spaghetti Monster. One of his tentacles reaches out to touch Adam's finger, with the tagline 'Touched by his noodly appendage'.

Such criticism of the traditional image of God is now widespread in our society. Young people especially regard such a critique as supporting their world-view and culture, and many of their idols, from comedians like Ricky Gervais and Eddie Izzard to TV celebrities like Derren Brown and Stephen Fry, affirm their views. For us to counter such misunderstanding and prejudice about the Christian God, we ourselves must embark on a liberative faith journey like the one taken by Celie in *The Color Purple*. By undertaking such a quest, we must aim to develop our image of God to reach a way of viewing the divine, and a way of speaking about the divine, that can make sense to the post-modern, scientific mindset, but still holds on to a theologically sound and time-honoured foundation. After all, such joviality about the Flying Spaghetti Monster hides a serious issue that Christians have to face. Traditionally, the Christian concept of God has been unashamedly other-worldly, and to the unbelieving mindset a supernatural God is increasingly seen as 'unbelievable'. At the foundation of this traditional, ethereal view of God, however, is not Christianity itself but rather the secular lens through which our faith has universally been read.

Casting off the Cartesian world-view

The first step in our journey of discovering an image of God that makes sense to an increasingly unbelieving world, then, is for us to recognize that certain philosophical and cultural movements in the past have been so pervasive in their influence on our faith that they have defined its very character. In its first few centuries, for example, Christianity found itself heavily influenced by Greek Platonic dualism, which differentiated starkly between the soul and the body. As a result of the influence of Platonism, Christian tradition has always reflected ambivalence towards physical matter. This is shown in our paradoxical attitude towards the body, which on the one hand is seen as the Temple of the Holy Spirit (1 Corinthians 6.19–20), and on the other hand is regarded as an obstacle to full union with Christ (Galatians 5.13–18).

Eighteenth-century Cartesian thought served merely to maintain these beliefs. Rene Descartes' 'I think therefore I am' philosophy affirmed the reality of our 'thoughts' and 'emotions', while doubting the experiences of our bodily senses. The physical world, then, became separated and alienated from us, and we began to identify more with our minds rather than with our bodies or the natural world. Cartesianism contributed to the development of modern scientific practice and method, which further disconnected us from the world around us. With the development of science, our universe became a machine to be studied objectively and impersonally, with the natural world viewed as a collection of predictable smaller machines, made up of isolated atoms. Whether we are studying science in school or at a more advanced level, rarely do we connect emotionally with what we study; rather, we distance ourselves from the world and view matter as a multiplicity of isolated and separated objects to be experimented upon. As Descartes himself asserted, 'I do not recognize any difference between the machines made by craftsmen and the various bodies that nature alone composes.'

Psychology, biology and the social sciences are all rooted in such a mechanistic view of the universe. Biology even uses the machine metaphor in its everyday vocabulary, employing phrases such as 'factories of cells', 'molecular machinery', 'assemblies of molecules' and 'DNA structures'. The human body itself has therefore been reduced to a machine, to be serviced occasionally and repaired by our doctors when faulty. Kazuo Ishiguro's dystopian view of the future in his novel *Never Let Me Go*, later adapted into an award-winning film with Keira Knightley and Carey Mulligan, is a sobering reflection on the possible consequences of this view of the physical world, as it paints a picture of a society where organ donation has reduced bodies to being, quite literally, machines to be harvested for 'parts'.

Within the scientific and medical community, however, many challenge the view of our bodies as having purely mechanical value. In my role as chaplain of Cardiff University, I visit the Biomedical School annually to officiate at a service over the cadavers used by the students in their study. The School has a policy that aims to make its medical students aware of the fact that these cadavers were once healthy, living bodies, with thoughts, feelings and emotions. Each student is asked to write a poem reflecting on the gift that these people have given – they have literally given their bodies so that others, who will be treated by these students in the future, may live.

Such attempts to redress the balance are commendable, but the prevailing contemporary attitude to the universe is that we are part of a lifeless, mechanistic and ultimately disaffected place. The Cartesian world is a world of alienation between body and mind, between person and person, and between human and nature. As a consequence, even society itself has become a machine to be studied by statistical models. Each one of us is a cog in this great machine, which the media and the advertising world are able to manipulate and influence. In the 2002 science-fiction film *Minority Report*, which sees Tom Cruise battling against the 'thought police', even the billboards on the roadside personalize the products that are advertised on them by scanning people's retinas as they walk past. And perhaps this unsettling vision of the future is not so distant a nightmare. Already our computers keep records of what we have bought and where we have been browsing on the internet; they will then, weeks or months later, advertise products similar to what we have earlier been perusing or purchasing. Advertisements for bikes for nine-year-old boys still appear on my computer, despite the fact that we have already bought a bike for my son and he is now 11 years old! In the cut-throat sphere of advertising, as elsewhere in our society, we are faced with an uncaring, controlling and competitive world, where there is little room for compassion, community and cooperation. Little wonder, then, that we live in a society of lonely, despairing and anxious souls.

God and the world

The prevalence of Platonism and Cartesianism in the history of the West has clearly had huge implications on present-day attitudes to the world around us. Thus our science, our politics and our economics all became unashamedly human-centred. For centuries, we insisted that humankind was quite literally at the centre of the universe, and scientists such as Johannes Kepler and Galileo Galilei were persecuted for suggesting that everything in our solar system revolves around the sun rather than around ourselves. While our science now recognizes that we are not so central to our universe, a general misplaced anthropocentricity continues to define our world-views. This has alienated us from nature and become a deeply ingrained attitude within most of us, tempting us to believe that we can own and control not only the objects around us but also the people, animals and nature. Such an individualistic and self-centred world-view, alongside our mechanistic view of the world, has led us to treat the earth as if it is a dead object. Sadly, our faith has become closely allied to this viewpoint, with God, rather than being the life force of creation we can recognize each day, becoming someone more distant on whom we call to intervene in times of crisis or for whom we put aside time each day or on Sunday to 'be with'.

While we may act in our daily lives as if we champion God's transcendence over his immanence, the reality is that most of us instinctively feel a deep affinity with the natural world and speak of it in deeply spiritual terms. In the retreats and quiet days that I lead, I very often ask about people's dreams, and especially what they would like to do before they die. The popular film *The Bucket List* (2007) brought this question to the public's attention, as two terminally ill men, played by Jack Nicholson and Morgan Freeman, try to accomplish a wish list of things they would like to do before they 'kick the bucket'. As in the film, most of the answers I get from people on retreat are not actually about doing some *thing*, but rather about visiting a *place*. These are often places of awe-inspiring natural beauty, somewhere people are either desperate to return to one more time after having been there in the past, or keen to visit because they have seen breathtaking pictures in books or spectacular footage on television. Most of us have somewhere in our hearts that we long to visit. I would personally love to return one more time to the countryside around Santa Fe in New Mexico, with its beautiful hummingbirds, scurrying salamanders and sweeping orange-tinted deserts. My wife, on the other hand, enthuses about visiting Yosemite National Park in California, being able to touch the ancient giant sequoia trees, witness the spectacular waterfalls, and hear the yapping of the wild coyotes. When we have such a desire to connect with the earth, whether we are dreaming about faraway places we would one day love to visit or simply looking forward to a trip to the local beach at the weekend or a walk in the park at lunchtime, we are reflecting a deeply spiritual longing – a memory of what we once had and a hope for what we will have in the future.

While we were visiting my parents' house in North Wales, my mother took my five-year-old daughter into the garden to help her with some jobs. I sat in the conservatory and watched them outside in the sunshine, spending two laughter-filled hours planting beans, watering flowers and putting out nuts for the birds. That evening, as I put my daughter to bed, she closed her eyes and clasped her hands together for her prayers. To my surprise, instead of the usual prayer, she said out loud, word for word: 'Dear Lord, The kiss of the sun for pardon, the song of the birds for mirth, one is nearer God's heart in a garden, than anywhere else on earth. Amen'! On enquiring where and when she had learned this little verse, she informed me that it was taught to her by Grandma that afternoon as they planted beans. My mother later told me that she had been taught this verse by her own grandmother after the war, when she used to help her in her garden. 'She told me that every garden is a little paradise, a hidden Eden,' my mother added. 'There is nowhere closer to the creator than his creation.'

In our hearts, many of us know that God's fingerprints can be found in nature, but as the history of Christianity unfolded our faith instead came to view the natural world with a great deal of disregard and even disdain, and the traditional reading of the Genesis story was used to uphold this theological framework. The creation of Adam was seen as the pinnacle of God's creative process, and so warped humankind's self-image. Spirituality and theology became unashamedly person-centred – and, if truth be told, largely man-centred. The rest of creation has therefore been reduced to a mere backdrop in the great theodrama being played out between humankind and God. We were certain that we were the crown of God's creation, the most important thing that he put here on earth. Salvation and redemption in Jesus, the second Adam, also became viewed in an anthropocentric and individualistic manner. As late as the 1980s, a primary school textbook on the Catholic faith was being used to teach children a hierarchy of God's love. *Christ's Life in Us*, written by Maria de la Cruz and Mary Richard, asks children to choose 'the one that God loves the most' by drawing a circle round one of the options on a diagram. In ascending order these options are: plants at the bottom, through animals in the middle, to baptized babies at the pinnacle of the diagram. Even if we were not directly taught of such a hierarchy, many of us who were brought up as Christians will recognize the attitude that the workbook exposes.

In his introduction to *The Green Bible*, Dave Bookless, the national director of A Rocha UK, laments that his church upbringing did not introduce him to a God who cared about the environment or our use of natural resources. Bookless asserts that God's word was read far too selectively by the churches in which he was involved. 'It's as if we put on special glasses which filtered out anything that wasn't about human beings and our relationship with God,' he recalls; 'just as sunglasses keep out ultraviolet rays, my mental processes were blanking out whole frequencies of biblical light.' Most of us would have to admit that we rarely hear preaching or teaching about the environment, ecology or the natural world in our churches. As such, our faith opens itself up to the accusation of being self-absorbed and blasé about the ecological crisis that humankind now faces. In the 1960s, a famous article appeared in *Science* magazine accusing Christianity of being at the root of our environmental predicament. 'Especially in its Western form,' wrote Lynn White in that article, 'Christianity is the most anthropocentric religion the world has seen.' White claimed that our faith is guilty of regarding itself as 'superior to nature, contemptuous of it, willing to use it for our slightest whim'. As late as the 1980s, James Watt, later to be US Secretary of the

Interior, wrote that 'the earth was put by the Lord for His people to subdue and to use for profitable purposes on their way to the hereafter'. Certainly much has changed for the better in the past 30 years, with many Churches and denominations issuing guidelines to help churches in their attitude to caring for God's creation, detailing information about environmental issues such as recycling, using renewable energy solutions and reducing pollution. However, an attitude of anthropocentric superiority remains in many quarters of the Church, even if only unconsciously. As Christians, we need to wake up to the fact that our collective survival is important to God, not merely our individual salvation. Thus in all of our church activity, from mission evangelism to social action, we should never disregard its impact on the natural world.

A bleakly individualistic and person-centred spirituality is, after all, alien to much of the Bible and to the spirituality that Jesus himself practises in the Gospels. Salvation is not merely about us as individuals, as even our destiny is bound up with the entire created order (Romans 8.18–25). Just as the fall of humankind involved the whole of creation, so the salvation of a new humanity in the second Adam carries with it the entire cosmos. Christ's work in bringing about such a cosmic reconciliation, however, has largely been replaced in Christian theology by an emphasis on individual human salvation. This is in stark contrast to the vast majority of biblical images of the end of the world. Most eschatological pictures in Scripture are unashamedly communal and often relate to the natural world. In the Old Testament, for example, we are given a picture of wonderful harmony in nature at the end of time, as the lion lives with the lamb, the leopard lies with the goat, and the small child peacefully leads all the creatures (Isaiah 11.6). This has significant implications for the way we relate now to each other and to the world around us. Edward Hicks' famous painting 'The Peaceable Kingdom' (*c*. 1833) presents Isaiah's future imagery of the harmony of nature alongside a scene of settlers and native

Americans in peaceful unity. In the New Testament, the images of the future kingdom are likewise communal and harmonious – the banquet, the wedding feast, the choir of all nations, and the New Jerusalem. To remain faithful to the biblical evidence, then, we cannot separate the destiny of the individual, the community and the entire created order. 'For by him all things were created,' writes St Paul to the Colossians (1.16–17), 'things in heaven and on earth, visible and invisible, whether thrones or powers or rulers or authorities; all things were created by him and for him. He is before all things, and in him all things hold together.'

Rather than being dualistic and individualistic, then, our faith should recognize that matter is not an enemy of spirit, but infinitely valuable to God. While 'materialism' as a world-view certainly runs counter to the Christian faith, there is no getting away from the fact that matter truly matters to God. In fact, the realization that we need not defend the barrier between spirit and matter can be an extremely liberating experience. After all, this is a false barrier, built and maintained by a Church temporarily blinded by secular philosophies. Through a rejection of dualism and individualism we can forge a holistic sense of spirituality, and thus affirm the created order. By doing so, we are inspired to treat it with the care, respect and love with which God himself treats it. Our faith can certainly not be regarded as 'universal' if we turn a blind eye to the universe itself.

2

Interconnectedness

———•◆•———

Apprehend God in all things, for God is in all things; every single creature is full of God, and is a book about God; every creature is a word of God.

Meister Eckhart

'I have ten thousand engagements of state today, but I would prefer to spend a day out here getting a wet arse, studying dandelions and marvelling at bloody spider's webs.' 'Have you found God, sir?' 'I think he found me.'

Ioan Gruffudd as William Wilberforce in
Amazing Grace *(2006)*

In the film *I Heart Huckabees* (2004), Dustin Hoffman waxes lyrical to Jason Schwartzman about the breathtaking interconnectedness of the universe. His description of the oneness of our world is both revealing and enlightening. He holds up a blanket and asks Schwartzman to imagine that it represents all the matter and energy in the universe. Every person, every animal, every plant, every object, every particle may be a different part of the blanket, he explains, but it is still part of the very same blanket. The problem comes when we see ourselves as separate from, or outside of, the blanket. 'Everything is the same, even if it is different,' comments Schwartzman. Hoffman enthuses at this conclusion: 'Exactly! Our everyday mind forgets this. We think everything is separate, limited. I'm over here, you're over there, which is true, but it's not the whole truth. Because we're all connected.' He ends with some pertinent advice: 'We need to see the blanket truth all the time – right in the everyday stuff.'

17

Our world is certainly connected in so many ways. This is true at a molecular level, but also at a more immediate level of our experience. 'We are caught in an inescapable network of mutuality, tied in a single garment of destiny,' Martin Luther King Jr wrote in a letter from his cell in Birmingham jail, Alabama, in 1963; 'whatever affects one directly, affects all indirectly.' Even at school we are taught how intimately inter-related we are to the rest of our world – our trees supply the oxygen for our survival, our weather dictates our water supplies, and insects pollinate the flowers and plants that we rely on for food. As such, interconnectedness is at the heart of the recent worldwide concern about the vanishing colonies of honey bees. It is estimated that bees pollinate two-thirds of all the world's fruits and vegetables. Furthermore, the growth of nuts and seeds is also reliant on bees, as is the cultivation of crops used as farm animal feed. Thus we would have very empty dinner tables without bees, as around one in every three bites of our entire diet is dependent on these small insects! The suggestion that the disappearance of the bees may be linked to our use of systemic pesticides on the crops that the bees pollinate, possibly interfering with their nervous systems and their ability to return to their hives, suggests further that nature and ourselves are inextricably reliant on each other. 'Honey bees are a sentinel of our environment, a modern canary in the coal mine,' suggested the 2009 award-winning documentary film *The Vanishing of the Bees*. 'Their sudden disappearance carries an important message.'

Interconnectedness and humankind

A number of Hollywood films have explored the interconnected-ness of the universe, especially in relation to our intimate bonds with each other. From the 1990s a series of box-office smashes, including *Two Days in the Valley* (1996), *Magnolia* (1999) and *Traffic* (2000), showed how our lives are intricately connected, despite the fact that often we do not consciously realize how they relate to each other. Even in our own everyday lives we often have moments when the interconnectedness of our lives takes us by surprise. Dinner-party conversations sometimes descend into stories of people who bump into their next-door neighbour while on holiday abroad or who travel to the far reaches of the earth only to find an old school friend staying in the same hotel. Furthermore, social networking sites like Facebook often reveal mutual friendships that leave us startled – 'How do you know *that* friend of mine?!' As early as 1929, Hungarian author Frigyes Karinthy suggested that you could take any two people in the world and connect them with each other through six steps or fewer. In other words, a chain of 'a friend of a friend' statements could be made between you and Barack Obama, just as it could be made between you and a factory worker living in Beijing in China. This has become known as the 'six degrees of separation' and has served to inspire films (*Six Degrees of Separation* (1993), starring Will Smith and Donald Sutherland), TV programmes (such as the *Lost* series (2004–10)) and popular music (including No Doubt's 'Full Circle'). Recent research has shown that our connection to each other may be even closer than the six degrees of separation thesis. In 2011, the BBC reported that researchers at the University of Milan had concluded, using the data of 721 million Facebook users, that there was, in fact, a mere 3.74 degrees of separation between us.

The succession of Hollywood films on the subject of interconnectedness in life pinnacled in two critically acclaimed box-office hits – the three-time Oscar winner *Crash* (2004, starring Sandra Bullock and Don Cheadle) and the seven-time Oscar-nominated *Babel* (2006, with Brad Pitt and Cate Blanchett). Both films show how very different and diverse lives are closely interrelated and how circumstances can lead our lives to weave seamlessly with each other. The titles of the films reveal the danger of ignoring the impact our actions have on the people and the world around us. *Crash* bemoans the consequences of being blind to the suffering of others, while *Babel* references the story of the Tower of Babel, where separateness is something the human race brings upon itself by its own hunger for power and knowledge.

From the book of Genesis onwards our faith has long recognized such a unity of everything, which finds its whole existence in God himself. Far from being new age nonsense or eastern mysticism, interconnectedness is at the heart of Christianity. All of us are in the process of becoming, but underneath that unsettling and constant change in our lives is the deep peace of a timeless Being. 'There is nothing created that does not contain a ray of God's radiance,' wrote Hildegard of Bingen, 'not foliage or seed or flower or any other beautiful creation.' God and his creation are, then, intricately and intimately connected, as the prologue of John's Gospel affirms (John 1.1–14). In a sense, creation flows out of God, and then exists within God. 'The day of my spiritual awakening,' wrote thirteenth-century contemplative Mechthild of Magdeburg, 'was the day when I saw, and understood that I saw, all things in God and God in all things.'

Interconnectedness and God

The Eastern Orthodox tradition describes a distinction between God's eternal and mysterious being that lies beyond our experience, and his 'divine energy' that infuses all creation, is recognizable in the world and is accessible to us. Prominent figures in the Western traditions have commented on this intimate interplay between God and his creation. 'God is in all things, yes he reigns in the very heart of all things,' asserted the great Catholic scholastic St Thomas Aquinas. Likewise, the Protestant reformer Martin Luther affirmed strongly that while God is greater than his creation, he also very much indwells in the universe. 'God is substantially present everywhere,' he wrote, 'in and through all creatures, in all their parts and places, so that the world is full of God and he fills all, but without his being encompassed and surrounded by it.' For the large part, though, such theologians were lone voices crying in the theological wilderness, so fearful were others of veering from the Platonic dualism of the early church, which saw matter and spirit in firm opposition.

Yet such a holistic view of the universe is actually a biblically ordained affirmation of the sacramental and incarnational role of the natural world. Christ has an independent identity from his creation, but he is also 'all, and in all' (Colossians 3.11). God is both transcendent and immanent, both *beyond* and *in* nature. As such, God is separate from creation and is certainly not dependent on his creation. But still, creation is the primary mode through which the Trinity chooses to disclose itself to us and relates to us.

The world around us is, then, fundamental to our under-standing of God, as it reveals his glory to us. The fathers of the early church wrote about animals praising God, even if these creatures were not aware of this fact. This same idea was recently expressed in the best-selling novel *The Shack*, written by William P. Young. In the secluded, peaceful place where the lead character would later actually meet God himself, he describes how the countryside drew him closer to the divine, despite the personal suffering he was undergoing:

> Of all the places he sensed the presence of God, out here surrounded by nature and under the stars was one of the most tangible. He could almost hear the song of worship they sang to their creator, and in his reluctant heart he joined in as best he could.

Nature actually reveals something of God, filling us with awe-inspired wonder and drawing us closer to the transcendent. In the early church, some thinkers related the natural world to Scripture itself, as the 'Word of God' was seen as revealed in both the Bible and in our everyday appreciation of the created order.

In the fourth century, St Anthony was asked how he could live a holy life in the desert, when he was so far away from books. 'My book is the nature of created things,' he answered, 'whenever I want to read the word of God, it is there before me.'

The Celtic saints likewise considered nature as holding an intrinsically close relationship with the divine. Although my family spoke English at home, my father used to encourage us children to pray in the Welsh language. He used to say, 'Prayer in English is sometimes beautiful, prayer in Welsh is always pure poetry.' As a child, therefore, I began to view Welsh as the language of prayer and worship; I would attend my dad's Welsh church and spend many an hour in his study devouring his books of ancient Celtic spiritual verse. From that poetry, it became clear to me that the early Celtic church saw very little division between heaven and earth, and they considered the veil between God and his creation to be slight. I still remember one Welsh poem from my dad's dusty library that reflects this fact. 'Offeren y Llwyn' ('The Woodland Mass'), by the fourteenth-century Welsh bard Dafydd ap Gwilym, may have been written some centuries after the old Celtic saints had lived, but it beautifully encapsulates their view of the world around them. The Cathedral in this poem is not made out of cold stone, it is the flourishing hedgerows and trees, brimming with precious life. The birds are presented as the singing priests with their colourful vestments, an old tree is the altar, the leaves are the wafers of bread, and the whole cosmos joins with the nightingale in singing 'with adoration to God the Father and with the chalice of ecstasy and love'. Ap Gwilym concludes that 'this psalmody pleases me: bred it was by a gentle grove of birch trees'.

Despite academic theology's reticence to recognize the interconnectedness of creation, such a deep respect for nature was not unusual in the popular theology of the Church by the Middle Ages. This was especially reflected in the Gothic architecture of the period. Nature bursts out of the stained-glass windows and the carved stones of the great European cathedrals – flowers, trees, animals, birds, insects, and even stars and planets. The word made flesh, the incarnation, not only told the medieval worshippers something about humankind, it also spoke about the whole cosmos. Hildegard of Bingen described God himself as a 'greening' power (*veriditas*), the divine life-force surging through the cosmos, creating and sustaining life. This power is both the foundation of all that exists and the glue that holds the universe together. Because of him, all parts of creation work in harmony and are intimately connected with each other.

As we have the very same source as every living thing, we are, therefore, in some way at one with the rest of the natural world. Pierre Teilhard de Chardin, the twentieth-century Jesuit palaeontologist, saw matter and spirit as intricately related, being two complementary facets of the same God. Thus creation is infused with, in his words, 'the spirit of fire'. A sense of being at one with God should, then, be at the very heart of experiences of interconnectedness. His involvement is part and parcel of the interdependent and interconnected web of life. God is the colour in life's rich tapestry.

Experiencing God

By recognizing this interconnectedness in creation we are drawn quite naturally to find God in the rich tapestry of our everyday experiences. There is an account (probably apocryphal) of a group of people shipwrecked off the coast of Brazil, who had survived by clambering aboard a raft. Although they were perishing of thirst, they failed to realize that they were, in fact, floating on fresh water. At the coast, a river was coming out into the sea with such force that the fresh water went out for a number of miles. They died, one by one, having no idea that the water all around them was drinkable. Similarly, our world is steeped in God's presence, dripping in God's glory and beauty, but so many of us fail to open our eyes to this fact. Karl Rahner, often referred to as a 'mystic of everyday life', pointed out that God's grace is active in all parts of creation, and thus his self-communication is present in the midst of our everyday lives – in the beautiful flowers of the hanging baskets that we pass each day, in the ladybird that lands on our lap in the park, in the smile of a shop assistant as she gives us our change, in the phone conversation with an old school friend, in the memories of times or people now long gone, in uplifting music on the radio, in the laughter of children in the playground, and in the stillness of silence.

We do not experience God in ways that take us out of this world, but we experience him in ways that root us even more deeply in the world. As we recognize and truly appreciate the wholeness of the world around us, it is as if, to use Hildegard of Bingen's description, we are being kissed by the divine life-force. But to achieve this we need continually to liberate our spirits from the Cartesian way that has taught us to view the world in a mechanistic and sterile manner. Young children connect so easily with a sense of wonder and amazement, and rarely dismiss things as being banal, mundane or trivial. Walt Whitman's paean to childhood, entitled 'There was a child went forth every day', is a poem that encapsulates this sense of awe that is innate to us all as children. It describes a child 'becoming' those things that it comes into contact with – not only the human influences in its life, but also flowers, grass, birds, animals, oceans, clouds, and even the horizon's edge.

> There was a child went forth every day;
> And the first object he look'd upon, that object
>   he became;
> And that object became part of him for the day.

Our aim as adults, then, should be to continue beholding God's creation as though we are viewing it for the very first time, so that the world becomes part of us, not just for a day but 'for many years, or stretching cycles of years'. As we are gradually introduced to more dualistic and mechanistic thinking, though, we become increasingly desensitized to the beauty and awe of life. It is certainly not science that blocks us from such a connection with life, as scientists often find that amazement increases with their scientific knowledge. Even Richard Dawkins speaks of his 'kind of religious reverence for the beauties of the Universe'. Rather, it is often our sense of separateness and our subsequent obsession with attaining objects and things for our individual satisfaction that blind us from day-to-day amazement at the world around us.

Experiences of oneness, of wholeness, of interconnectedness, and of feeling at home in the world, in fact, cross boundaries of time, geography and culture. Sometimes, as with Buddhism, these experiences are interpreted non-theistically. In the Christian contemplative tradition, however, a sense of being at one with God has accompanied such experiences. Still, in recent years the whole question of religious experience has become increasingly sidelined and obscure among the majority of young people. Very few of the young people with whom I work are comfortable about talking openly about any so-called 'religious' experience. This, of course, does not mean that people today have ceased to have such experiences. It points, rather, to the fact that we tend to frame and explain such occurrences in a very different way from how we might have done in the past.

Incidences in my own past have brought this fact home to me. As Colin Firth puts it in the Oscar-nominated *A Single Man* (2009):

A few times in my life I've had moments of absolute clarity, when for a few brief seconds the silence drowns out the noise and I can feel, rather than think. And things seem so sharp, and the world seems so fresh. It's as though it had all just come into existence . . . I've lived my life on these moments. They pull me back to the present. And I realize that everything is exactly the way it's meant to be.

My earliest memories of such moments are of when I used to lie in bed at the dead of night, with the curtains open, marvelling at the stars. I felt strangely in touch with them, despite their being light years away, and they helped me feel at home in an increasingly uncertain world by the reassurance of their presence each clear night. No words can explain the awe and wonder felt by my whole being as I gazed upwards. Likewise, no words were involved in the experience itself – just a rooting in the present moment that led me to feel that those heavenly bodies and I were, in some way, one and the same. Years later, in my mid twenties, I was driving through West Wales while a terrible storm raged all around. I was forced to brake sharply as a flash flood submerged the road in front of me. As I watched the amazing power of nature surging past, my reaction was not fear, and again did not involve thought or words; I was instead filled with a profound sense of clarity, joy and amazement. And recently, I attended a U2 concert in the Millennium Stadium in Cardiff. During the concert a short clip of an interview with Desmond Tutu was relayed on a huge screen. The ageing Archbishop reminded the audience of the absolute centrality of love in any and every situation. As the picture faded away, U2 began to sing their hit single 'One', with its emphasis on the power of love to bring unity and wholeness. Again, I felt myself being taken back to that same feeling I had when I looked at the stars as a child, and when I sat trapped in the flash flood a decade ago. This was a feeling of awe, a feeling of warmth, and a palpable feeling of oneness with everything around me – at one with all the others in the audience, as well as at one with the stars above me, peering down through the stadium's open roof. Most strangely of all, in these three experiences (and many further similar experiences) I almost felt indestructible, as if no real harm could befall me. I was at one with all creation and with the ground of all creation, and all was at one with me.

These kinds of experiences are not unique to me, and they are certainly not due to any exceptional connection that I possess with the transcendent. Everyone faces similar experiences, yet to communicate such complex incidents with others is immensely difficult. In centuries gone by, these experiences would have been described soaked in religious and spiritual terminology: 'A light filled my whole being with grace and joy, and I heard a reassuring voice from the heavens, "I am the light of the world, and I will lead you safely out of your darkness – I will not forsake you".' In today's society, however, such mystical explanations would be taken too literally, and any talk of hearing voices would raise serious questions with regard to mental health issues. The use of such language, then, has to be treated with great care, and we are often left to struggle with the confines of twenty-first-century language and, sometimes, with our own embarrassment of such experiences.

Etty Hillesum, before her incarceration and eventual death at Auschwitz, suggested that almost all people have moments when they feel at one with the creative and cosmic forces of the world. She describes how she felt such moments herself when she was listening to inspiring music or when she was lying on her bed and looking out at the wonder of nature from her window. 'Truly,' she wrote, 'it does feel as if I were clinging to the earth herself and not to a genuinely bourgeois, soft and decadent mattress.' Yet even she admits that, as early as the 1940s, it took great courage to label these uplifting moments as 'God'.

Perhaps, then, one of our faith's roles in today's society is to affirm such experiences, as one of our greatest gifts is that we can provide a language to frame such 'encounters'. Such a language need not be overly 'religious', theological or mystical. We sometimes believe that any experience of the transcendent has to be couched in a supernatural vocabulary or at least has to use the same terminology that our ancestors used. There is a popular story of a Sunday school teacher trying to inspire the children to recognize the divine in the natural world around them. She asked the children to guess what she was thinking of, and gave them clues such as, 'it has a bushy tail', 'it enjoys running around', and 'it collects nuts'. One child quickly retorted, 'Well, it sounds like a squirrel, but I know that the answer must be Jesus.' The ways of talking about God for one generation sometimes become staid and outdated by the next generation. We should certainly not be throwing out traditional language, but rather opening our minds and our hearts to new ways of talking about our moments of connection with something that is bigger than ourselves.

Such a realization is part of the move from a concept of God as an otherworldly figure to an experience of him embedded in creation. While the concept of a transcendent God who is radically other should not be disregarded, our principal mode of experiencing God is in our relationships with all that seem 'other' to us, but are actually one with us. God is certainly much more than his creation, but our own experience of him is still very much bound up with his creation.

As well as providing a vocabulary, the Church should be offering practical opportunities for us to connect with the transcendent in our everyday lives. This is principally a process of prompting a recognition that just as the traditional separation of body and mind or matter and spirit is a falsehood, the separation of secular and religious is ultimately false. Yet in the contemporary world both 'sides' jealously guard their separate and distinctive natures. On the one hand, the Church continues to refer to 'the secular world'. It still maintains a dichotomy between those within the body of Christ and those 'outside the Church'. On the other hand, the so-called 'secular world' remains greatly embarrassed by the concept of faith. Practising Christians often keep their faith hidden from colleagues and even friends, and outward admissions of faith are frequently seen as signs of weakness, quirkiness or even lunacy. A striking example of this attitude was witnessed when the former British Prime Minister Tony Blair attempted to talk about his Christian faith in an interview with *Vanity Fair*. His communications manager

Alastair Campbell immediately stopped the interviewer's questions. 'We don't do God,' was Campbell's now famous retort.

The Christian God is, however, the ground of the being of the whole world, and not simply the ground of each of us as individuals. He is integral to existence as a whole and he is connected to every single aspect of our lives and of the life of the world. Nothing is secular. As such, we must open our eyes to the involvement of God in our work, our politics and our relationships. This is not an authoritarian involvement, where God provides rules for us to obey or controls each and every event that takes place. Rather, his involvement is bound up in the interconnectedness of life and in the daily relationships we foster with the world around us. After all, while a service on Sunday may be important to many of us, it accounts for only a very short time of our hectic week. We aim, therefore, to open our eyes to God in the daily routines of the rest of our week. Church does not start and finish on Sunday, but continues in whichever community God has placed us. Whether we are a nurse, a shop assistant, a lawyer, or a teacher, God has placed us to be salt and light in our communities. As we work, socialize and relax, we must recognize that the secular and the spiritual are as one in our lives, undivided and in harmony.

3

Relationship

———•••———

There is no such thing as society. There are individual men
and women and there are families.
> *Margaret Thatcher in* Woman's Own *magazine (1987)*

> Only *one* space extends
> Through all beings: innerworldspace.
> Silently, the birds fly within us.
> And I, who wants to grow, I look outside,
> But find *within* me grows the tree.
> > *Rainer Maria Rilke,*
> > *'Nearly everything calls us to connect'*

The 2010 documentary film *Dreams of a Life* is a compassionate
reflection on the life and death of 38-year-old Joyce Vincent.
In 2006 she was found dead in her London flat, surrounded by
her unopened Christmas presents and with her television still
switched on. Her body had remained undetected for over two
years. During her short life she was a vivacious and popular
woman, but she died alone and was apparently unmissed by
her family, friends and colleagues. 'The debate about living
in dislocated societies, not having communities any more,' noted
the journalist who first reported that Vincent's decomposed
body had been found, 'it's been banging on for ages and it's
just been a sort of theory; and this is the living reality of it.'
An article in *The Guardian* newspaper shortly after the release
of *Dreams of a Life* suggested that Joyce Vincent's situation was
not unique. It listed a handful of similar cases and highlighted
the fact that in 2007 the charity Help the Aged reported that

hundreds of thousands of elderly people in the UK have few, if any, visitors, and in a poll more than a million said that they were often or always lonely. Further research undertaken internationally in 2012 by the charity WRVS compared the UK to other countries and concluded that elderly Britons were the loneliest and most neglected in Europe, with many going for weeks without any contact. 'This research highlights the sad truth about growing old in Britain today,' claimed the chief executive of the charity, 'and should act as a wake-up call.'

This situation certainly reflects how individualistic and isolated society has become. The 'I' has become far more important than the 'we', and we rarely take other people into account as we go about our everyday lives. In 2004, *New Statesman* columnist Martin Jacques bemoaned the 'age of selfishness' in which we live by employing quasi-religious terminology. 'The credo of self,' he wrote, 'inextricably entwined with the gospel of the market, has hijacked the fabric of our lives.' At a more basic level, a recent advertisement on our TV screens proudly shows all of us living on our own little planets, leaving our homes only to take little spaceships to visit other people on their own lonely little planets. We are all portrayed as separated, detached and disconnected. The most disconcerting thing is that to most of us this portrayal seems not only innocuous, but positively desirable. After all, we are taught from an early age, either consciously or unconsciously, that detachment is something for which we should aim. It may even seem to us that the more successful we are, the more we earn the 'privilege' of privacy. We may well begin our adult lives in a terraced house, but then we work hard so that we can 'upgrade' to a semi-detached house. Then our dream is to purchase a detached house. If money is no issue, we might then buy a house with a large garden surrounding it, separating us from our neighbours. Worse still, for security reasons we might then erect large fences and gates around our shiny new house, which shut us in and shut the rest of the world out.

In our workplaces, too, our aim is to move from the open-plan office where many of us start our careers, and in which we are forced to actually engage directly with our colleagues, to a shared office with one or two others. Finally, we hope to be promoted to a snug private office, separated from the hoi polloi. Richard Fuld, the CEO of Lehman Brothers before its collapse in 2008, never himself appeared on the trading floor. He even had his own private elevator to get to his office. His driver would call his security guard in the morning to confirm the elevator was ready. This ensured that there would be, in the words of Lawrence McDonald, the former vice president of the company, 'only a two or three second window where he actually had to see people'. He would then quickly hop out of his private car and into his lift, which took him directly to his office on the thirty-first floor. 'Fuld went out of his way to be disconnected,' recalls McDonald in the documentary film *Inside Job* (2010).

We are increasingly distancing ourselves from each other, as 'community' and 'society' are being eroded and new and impersonal methods of communication are bringing even further disconnectedness from our neighbours. Our faith, however, should instil in us a very different attitude in our lives. After all, relationship, community and society are at the very heart of Christianity. We are not called to be alone or detached, and certainly not to be preoccupied with our own well-being. Rather, we are called to recognize our mutual dependence on one another and on the world around us. At the very core of this interconnectedness is God himself, who is relentlessly trying to lure us into oneness with him and his creation. Many non-Christians recognize this sense of unity that binds all life, although they rarely relate it to God's transcendence. 'She talks about a network of energy that flows through all living things,' muses Sam Worthington in the Oscar-winning film *Avatar* (2009), 'she says all energy is only borrowed, and one day you have to give it back.' In 2008, the writer and environmental activist Alistair McIntosh received a grant from the World Wildlife Foundation to research the spirituality of rural and urban regeneration. He concluded that the bond that connects people, place and nature is very much related to the ineffable. For Christians, then, God is at the very heart of the relationship between all living things and this realization has huge implications for our ethics and values.

Relationship and faith

I walked into my young daughter's bedroom recently to find her sitting alone, staring at a glass of orange juice on her small desk. When I asked her what she was doing, she replied that she was trying to move the glass by looking at it. 'I often try to move things with my mind,' she said, 'but, so far, it's just not working.' Her lack of success is, of course, not surprising – the physical world has definite laws and rules that are, on the face of it, impossible to break. The 2009 film *The Men Who Stare at Goats* explores the possibility that we can indeed master techniques to manipulate the physical world. Starring George Clooney and Ewan McGregor, it is loosely based on Jon Ronson's book on the US Army's apparently true-life exploration of possible military applications of new age and paranormal concepts. Almost all the techniques investigated are fanciful and farcical, to say the very least – there are attempts to kill goats by the power of the mind, run through solid walls, and separate clouds by concentrating on them. What underlies these efforts, however, is an innate intuition held by numerous people down the ages that all matter is somehow intimately connected. Moving objects with our minds or walking through solid walls are clearly impossible ventures, but our desire to do so may, in fact, reflect a very real oneness with the world around us.

The narrative in Genesis 1 gives credence to the view that there is unity and harmony to every part of God's creation. The Hebrew word for 'man' (*adam*) is closely related to the word for 'soil' or 'ground' (*adamah*). From our very inception, then, we were part and parcel of nature itself, made from soil and destined to return to soil. God animates this soil with the 'breath of life' (*neshamah*), a phrase used in the Old Testament to express his gift of granting both human and non-human life (cf. Job 37.10). We therefore share a deep intimacy both with God himself and with all other living things, a reality reflected in the fact that nature and the natural world figure so prominently in Christ's parables and miracles.

In the past, spirituality and theology have been very much person-centred, with the theo-drama between humankind and God sidelining the rest of creation. Thus our faith, alongside every other area of our lives (such as politics and economics), has developed as unashamedly anthropocentric. Yet in Genesis, everything is created before humans are called into being – wind, water, earth, air, fish, birds and animals. When we are finally formed, we are created for being in relation to, and being together with, both God and the world around us. 'In the beginning was the relationship,' asserted Martin Buber. At the time of Noah, that relationship is cemented through a covenant that is made not only with humankind but with all living things. The concept of covenant is fundamental to both the Old and New Testaments, shown in the fact that even the word 'testament' is from the Latin word for covenant (*testamentum*). At the heart of covenant is God's continual relationship with his creation, echoed throughout Scripture in the fact that he truly cares about each part of the cosmos. 'The LORD is good to all,' asserts Psalm 145.9, 'he has compassion on all he has made.'

Our relationships with the world around us, then, echo God's essential being. Martin Buber claims that whenever we are engaged in the process of relationship, whether with other human beings or with animals and plants, we are connecting with the transcendent in our lives. God *is* relationship, and the concept of the Trinity brings this home forcefully to us. As Uncle Screwtape scowls in C. S. Lewis' *Screwtape Letters*, 'He claims to be three as well as one, in order that this nonsense about Love may find a foothold in His own nature.' Yet not only does the Trinity demonstrate that God himself is, in his very essence, in continual loving relationship with *himself*, it shows that he is also in continual relationship with *his creation*. Teilhard de Chardin suggested that the Trinity's internal life is very much bound up in all matter, and he argued that even the scientific process known as evolution reflects the Trinity itself, being a movement towards God the Creator, through his Son Christ, in the Holy Spirit. Centuries earlier, Hildegard of Bingen had suggested a similar infusion of the Trinity in creation. Yet, she claimed, many of us still fail to recognize the wonder of the divine in the natural world. 'Who is the Trinity?' she asked. 'You are music. You are life. You are alive in everything, yet you are unknown to us.' The Holy Spirit, according to Hildegard, is at the heart of this process, as he is the way that the Father and the Son bring the interconnectedness of existence into being. 'You are the mighty way,' she wrote in a prayer to the Holy Spirit, 'in which everything that is in the heavens, on the Earth and under the earth is penetrated with connectedness, is penetrated with relatedness.'

Science and theology in harmony

The intimate relationship between us and the world in which we live should, then, be central to our faith. If our Christian world-view is to connect with the contemporary world, however, it also needs to be rooted in science. During the past century, the mechanistic world-view of Descartes and Newton has been superseded within various scientific disciplines by a more holistic attitude. Increasingly, scientists are moving from a paradigm that sees the universe as a mechanical system, made up of a disconnected collection of parts, to a paradigm that regards the world as an integrated whole. The scientific approach entitled 'systems thinking' especially views all objects as part and parcel of their context, as everything is recognized to be connected intimately and involved in a complex system of living relationships. At a very basic level, for example, a tree is itself a network of connections, between the leaves, the branches, the bark, the roots, and so on. It then has numerous relationships with the world around it, with the soil, the weather, the wildlife living in its branches. Finally, a tree is also part of a greater network of relationships, for example the forest in which it is located or its local environment.

Thus there is an increasing recognition in science of a fundamental interdependence in nature. Even at the quantum level, atoms and subatomic particles are not viewed as isolated building blocks, but rather as complex and living relationships between the parts that make up the whole. These particles even continue communication with each other long after they have been separated. As Henry Stapp, one of the world's leading experts in quantum mechanics, puts it: 'An elementary particle is not an independently existing unanalysable entity. It is, in essence, a set of relationships that reach outward to other things.'

What contemporary science offers here is a shift from an emphasis on 'objects' to the recognition that 'relationship' is integral to the world around us. After all, if all the separate parts of a car were heaped in a pile on the floor, then no one would claim that was a car – we would conclude that it is simply a pile of rubbish for the scrap yard. Yet if someone were to arrange the parts in a particular order and the parts begin to interact with each other, we would immediately recognize it to be a car. But any mismatch between the parts will affect the harmony and balance of the engine, and the vehicle will subsequently start to be unreliable and might even break down. So it is with the world – the purpose and function of the natural world depends on every object's relationship with each other and with the whole, and that 'whole' is much more than the sum of its parts.

Seeing ourselves in the world around us

Science is increasingly revealing that relationship is integral to the make-up of the world around us. Interconnectedness is at the heart of everything. Cosmology and evolution suggest that all that exists has a common origin and all matter has an interrelated story over the past 14 billion years. The world is one large household, with everything in it having a place and a purpose. The Greek word for household is *oikos* – the root of the word 'ecology'. As in Genesis, the scientific discipline of ecology holds that our very breath of life is at the mercy of our relationships with the rest of the created order. Not only are we integral parts of an interdependent planetary system, but without the intricacies of our own ecosystem our lives could not be supported in the first place. Our atmosphere, and therefore our very existence, depends entirely on a symbiotic relationship between living creatures, plants and micro-organisms.

We are, then, bound up in an ongoing relationship and dialogue, not only with each other but with the plethora of everyday things we experience in our world – the sun, trees, flowers, animals, and so on. Even at a quantum level, the entire fabric of all that exists is woven so closely that everything is intricately related in a tangible way. Every particle has at some time worked with every other particle, and the destiny of each and every particle is therefore connected with the entire universe. 'Everything is connected, everything matters,' suggests Dustin Hoffman in *I Heart Huckabees*. 'There's not an atom in our bodies that's not been forged in the furnace of the sun. Isn't that cool?' As such, even the boundaries between different objects are blurred. At what point, for example, does the oxygen that we breathe into our bodies cease to be part of the air and become part of us? And do the bacteria that I ingest in my yoghurt drinks each morning become part of me, or are they separate from me? The reality is that everything in the world interacts seamlessly with everything else. All created things are intimately connected with each other. As Malcolm Hollick of the Findhorn Community writes, 'Molecules which yesterday were carrots and cows, are parts of me today.'

Our relationship with the rest of creation is certainly constant and profound, even if sometimes we feel detached and separate. Our species is, after all, utterly dependent on other creatures and on the world around us. This was true of our evolutionary origins, it is true of our present existence, and will be true of our future. We all came from the same particle, and we will all return to that same particle. We came from dust, and to dust we will return. It is in this sense that contemplatives down the centuries have made the remarkable deduction that we literally *are* each other. In other words, when something happens to you, it happens to me also, like the Siamese twins in the French film *The City of Lost Children* (1995) – as one inhales on a cigarette, the other breathes the smoke out. The futility and repugnancy of war are even more marked when we recognize that we are not killing each other when we take other lives, we are killing ourselves. This idea is reflected in the popular 1960s folk anthem 'Universal Soldier', written by Buffy Sainte-Marie and covered by Donovan, Joan Baez and Johnny Cash. According to the song there are not thousands of soldiers, fighting for different sides. Rather, there is one 'universal soldier', who is tall and short, Christian and atheist, old and young. Many years earlier, the French Cistercian contemplative Charles de Foucauld had suggested a similar concept of the 'universal brotherhood'. In other words, all of us are intimately connected as in one large family and we should treat each other with this in mind. As Archbishop Desmond Tutu put it: 'I hope we can accept a wonderful truth – we are family! We are family! If we could get to believe this we would realize that care about "the other" is not really altruistic, but it is the best form of self-interest.'

The concept of a universal brotherhood also has significant implications for our relationship with nature and our environment. It is only a small step from the recognition that we all have an intimate bond with each other to appreciating that we are also in a living relationship with the entire world around us. The contemplatives, for example, talk about losing themselves, not only in *everyone* but also in *everything*. We look at the living world around us, and rather than seeing separate and alien objects, we see ourselves. The Holocaust survivor Viktor Frankl describes how one young prisoner at Auschwitz, who knew she had only days left to live, began to feel a palpable sense of harmony with her surroundings. Pointing to a chestnut tree, she told Frankl that she often talked to that tree. He asked her if the tree, with its scattered blossoms, ever replied. 'Yes,' she answered, 'it said to me, "I am here – I am here – I am life, eternal life".'

We humans are part and parcel of the wonderful web of life, and even the simple objects in the environment around us, such as plants, flowers, pets, trees or birds, can become symbols to us of the joyous unity within our vast universe. Such living things are not, therefore, merely entities that are 'useful' to us, they are things that hold value and significance in themselves. If we can relate our own self to the world around us, and not cling so rigidly to our separate identities, then we are drawn naturally into a compassion towards all living things. 'Care flows naturally if the "self" is widened and deepened,' writes philosopher Arne Naess, 'so that protection of free nature is felt and conceived as protection of ourselves.' No longer, then, do we dismiss our world as something cheap and disposable, to be controlled and manipulated. Rather, the world is recognized for what it is – a finely tuned, growing organism, full of vitality and life. God, in return, expects us to extend his limitless love towards all of his creation, without exception.

The fallacies of separateness and uniformity

In our everyday lives, however, rather than recognizing the interconnectedness of life we are often drawn to revel in our separation from each other and from the rest of the world. At a very basic level, television shows such as *The Jeremy Kyle Show* and *The X Factor*, for example, fail to acknowledge our unity and common humanity, but instead rejoice in our dissimilarity with those we are watching. We almost delight in watching the 'rejects' of these shows, enjoying the feeling that we are so very different from them. Our enjoyment at the appalling vocal performances of contestants in the early auditions for *The X Factor*, or the inarticulate and poorly educated guests on *The Jeremy Kyle Show*, helps to make us feel better personally, but always at the expense of the weak, powerless or ignorant.

Still, there is something deep inside us that decries division and longs for oneness and harmony. Our obsession with sex in the western world reflects something of this. After all, two 'become one flesh' in sexual union is a phrase used in Scripture (Genesis 2.24 and Mark 10.8) that is frequently taken up in popular song lyrics, most famously by the Spice Girls in their smash hit 'Two Become One' from 1996. Likewise, the safety of the group mentality reflects this desire to be at one with others. This is most potently reflected in the popularity of nationalistic feelings. In my own country of Wales, the founders of the Welsh Nationalist Party (now known as Plaid Cymru) in the 1920s had a desire for unity and oneness that went beyond mere geographical boundaries. As a result, many of them converted to Roman Catholicism and announced their desire for Wales to become united under 'one country, one language, and one faith'. Paradoxically, such a desire for nationalistic unity on the one hand suggests a deep-seated hunger for relationship and solidarity, while on the other it defines itself against 'the other' and so can lead to the opposite of true unity and harmony. Thus our innate desire for unity can lead to division and to violence against those who do not share, for example, our same nationality, world-view, religion or even the same football team.

While our longing for unity can sometimes be distorted, there can be no doubt that deep in our nature is a desire for unity and acceptance. Isolation is devastating to the human psyche, which is why solitary confinement is regarded as the worst punishment for prisoners. It must be recognized, however, that unity does not mean uniformity. When we marry the person we love, for example, we should not lose our individual identities. A recent news report asked an elderly couple what was the secret of their long marriage. 'Just say "yes dear" a lot,' came the answer from the beleaguered husband! In reality, of course, marriages should be rooted in a depth of unity that allows freedom for both individuals. In February 2012 the British national press delighted in the tale of the country's oldest married couple joining the social networking site Twitter to help solve the relationship dilemmas of the young. The advice that Lionel and Ellen Buxton gave over Twitter was revealing, if predictable. Their romance, it seems, had lasted over 80 years because the support they offered to each other had allowed them to flourish both together and individually, and their personalities had shone as a result of the depth of intimacy and unity that marriage offered. Diversity within togetherness, then, is absolutely vital in our lives, and distinctive characteristics should not be lost through our recognition of the interconnectedness of life.

Since its very early years in the early twentieth century, the ecumenical movement among the churches, which again has the Greek word for household, *oikos*, at its root, has been through a similar journey of recognition in this regard. At first, many within this movement saw the ultimate aim of ecumenism as uniformity of doctrine and practice. Today, however, the vast majority of ecumenists view 'unity' as meaning a true harmony and union of individual denominations, all valued for what their distinctiveness brings to the worldwide Church, in the same way as all members of our literal households are loved for who they are and what they bring to our family units.

In a wider context, too, safeguarding our individuality should certainly not stop us embracing our mutual oneness, both with the world around us and with the divine source of the world.

This concept of diverse harmony within relationships is at the foundation of nature's interconnectedness. My wife is a choreographer, and she often waxes lyrical about the importance of harmony in her pieces. A dance, after all, is not merely one pose, and the music that accompanies a dance is not merely one note: a dance is a coordinated series of diverse physical movements, performed to a range of musical notes, which are set in harmony with one another. Diversity is integral to harmony. In the context of nature, we can recognize the beauty and richness of its diversity (in other words, its individual parts), but we should never ignore their harmonious relationship with each other. A leaf is a magnificent creation in itself, but we must also appreciate it in the context of the tree on which it grew. We can appreciate the distinctiveness of a tree, but also value it in the context of the forest in which it grows. Likewise the forest is to be celebrated as beautiful, but needs to be appreciated in the context of its wider landscape and environment. Thus we can recognize the wonderful uniqueness of every different phenomenon, while still maintaining that the whole is at the heart of ultimate reality.

Relationship, words and God

The Cartesian method of viewing and studying the world encourages us to be objective and disconnected from the world around us. Both our faith and contemporary science, however, suggest that it is relationship and oneness that are at the heart of the created order; by ignoring this we miss not only the reality of existence but also the richness of life. This does not mean, of course, that all forms of relationship are intrinsically good. Far too often in our westernized, capitalist world, relationships are rooted in control, consumerism and ownership. Both in nature and in the sphere of human relations, this leads to disorder and devastation, just as much as division and disjunction does. By reflecting God's essential being in our interactions, however, we step outside the distorted values of culture and society, and thus our relationships with the world around us will begin to reflect unity and compassion. After all, true relationship is not about commanding, manipulating and ruling; rather, it is about standing alongside the 'other' in a reciprocal love that allows both us and them to grow and flourish. Like the relationship of a flower with the soil beneath, this is a life-giving mutuality.

Likewise, our relationship with the divine should reflect this fact. Connecting with a God who is part and parcel of the world allows us to move away from the powerful, judgemental and demanding Deity Christians have been saddled with in the past, and to move towards the God of union, love and harmony. A God who is limited by our traditional ideas of almightiness and domination makes for a very one-sided relationship with his creation. Theology has traditionally referred to our affiliation with the divine in words that give us a passive, and even negative, role – God 'controls', 'uses', 'judges', 'sends', 'rules', and so on. This ignores the fact that Scripture, and much of the subsequent contemplative tradition, is saturated in non-hierarchical and liberating language. As a result, our spirituality and our worship can move towards these less authoritarian words, which are far more attuned to our contemporary mindset – we are 'nurtured', 'liberated' and 'inspired', and we can 'listen', 'participate' and 'experience'. Similarly, phrases such as 'water of life', 'light of the world' and 'life-giving spirit' enhance our appreciation of a consensual relationship with the transcendent, with each other, and with the world around us.

This does not mean, of course, that traditional images are simply discarded. In fact, many such images still hold much potency for us when they are defined in a life-affirming and holistic manner. When we pray the prayer Christ taught us, for example, we begin by calling God our 'Father'. By referring to the divine in this way, we are actually making a statement about our neighbours just as much as about God. If God is our father, then our neighbours are our universal brothers and sisters, as Charles de Foucauld put it. Love of God and love of neighbour are not separate dimensions of our spiritual lives: they are two sides of the same coin. In other words, our relationship with the divine will deepen our relationships with each other, and likewise, when we recognize our solidarity with one another we tread on divine ground.

Our relationship with God does not, however, merely impact our human experience; it is rooted in our relationships with the entire created order. To truly know someone, we don't study them from a distance and collect information about them. Rather, we enter into relationship with them. This is true of God, it is true of each other, and it is true of the world around us. We cannot really know nature from an objective study of it, but must be ready to immerse ourselves in it and encounter it directly. By doing so, we also encounter God directly and this will inspire us to become what he intended us to be – beings who care for and nurture God's creation. Roald Dahl's classic children's novel *Fantastic Mr Fox* presents all animals as united, working together against a common enemy – humankind. This image is obviously not to be taken literally, as there is much blood spilt between species. However, it does allude to a deeper truth about life. The fact remains that only humankind remains a threat to all species. Yet by affirming the oneness of all that exists, in all its diversity, distinctiveness and beauty, we are able to stand alongside God in his compassionate care for his creation. 'God desires that all the world be pure in his sight,' wrote Hildegard of Bingen; 'the Earth should not be injured, the Earth should not be destroyed.'

4

Bringing Jesus down to earth

God is inside you and inside everybody else. You come into
the world with God. But only them that search for it inside
find it. Sometimes it just manifest itself even if you not
looking, or don't know what you looking for.

Alice Walker, The Color Purple

> Christ has no body now but yours,
> No hands, no feet on earth but yours,
> Yours are the eyes with which he looks
> compassion on this world.
> Christ has no body now on earth but yours.
>
> *St Teresa of Avila*

In 1956 the poet Edwin Muir published 'The Incarnate One', a
poem that reflected on how Christians had subverted the good
news of the gospel. For Muir, the incarnation, the act of God
becoming human in the person of Jesus, had freed the divine to
be truly part of this physical universe. Yet instead of celebrating
that fact, Christians down the ages imprisoned him again in
the world of books and words. The wonder and mystery of God
are reduced to stagnant ideological arguments. This 'fleshless
word' can only distance humanity from the transcendent, and
it is almost as if the Fall is taking place all over again. Thus,
rather than us locating the presence of God in the world around,
we incarcerate him in our ideas and in our laws. Muir concludes
that, by today, the Word made flesh 'is made word again'.

The incarnation, then, challenges the dualisms that Platonism
left entrenched in our faith and it demands that we recognize
the inherent value of our earthly life and of the world around

45

us. This is very much in line with the rest of Scripture. After all, the goodness of creation is affirmed by God himself in the Genesis narrative (Genesis 1.31), the body is described as a temple of the Holy Spirit by St Paul (1 Corinthians 6.19), and the biblical vision of the future includes the resurrection of the body (1 Corinthians 15) and the creation of a new earth (Revelation 21.1). Still, in the 2,000 years of its history, Christianity has failed to live true to this theology. Today even the very word 'incarnation' is out of favour in some church traditions. While I was teaching recently, one student stopped the lecture to ask me the meaning of 'incarnation'. He later confessed that he had not heard the word in his own church and feared that I was talking about Buddhist reincarnation! Yet far from being alien to our faith, a belief in the 'incarnation' is so integral to Christianity that it could well be argued that belief in the incarnation is what actually makes a Christian a Christian. All theists believe in a God, but only Christians believe that God walked among us in physical form and, indeed, can still be found in the world around us.

Without an emphasis on the Christian incarnation our faith misses a fundamental element that is unmistakable in Scripture. St Lawrence Justinian was so influenced by the pervasive Platonism in the Church that he is said to have abstained from spending time in the countryside or in his garden, so certain was he that 'things of the world' were unhelpful to his spiritual life. In the twentieth century, Pierre Teilhard de Chardin claimed that the entire Church, by ignoring the incarnation and overlooking God's creation down the centuries, had become too insular and preoccupied with its own structure and worship rites. Jesus, he suggested, needed to be rescued from the Church 'so that the world can be saved'. Certainly, a wonderful consequence of the 'word made flesh' is that the Word (the *logos*) continues to be engaged in a constant and dynamic relationship with the world around us. It may, indeed, be tempting for us to regard God as only having resided in human form for a brief 33 years, before he ascended to heaven, leaving the Holy Spirit as a less physical manifestation of himself. But we must always remind ourselves that, as a song from the Guatemalan pop singer Ricardo Arjona puts it, in the incarnation God became a verb, rather than a noun (*Dios es verbo, no sustantivio*). Furthermore, that verb must never remain in the past tense. Even in the famous passage in John's Gospel that maintains that 'the Word became flesh' (John 1.14), the Gospel writer uses a Greek tense (the inceptive aorist) that implies an action that has started in the past but is continuing into the present. The phrase might rather be translated as 'the Word started to become flesh'. Thus, the Word continues to become flesh, even today.

Christ in us – the body of Christ today

The incarnation is certainly something that is at the very heart of the Christian faith. It has profound implications on our theology, and consequently on our everyday lives. First, the incarnation means that we, as Christians, must share the life of Christ – by laughing when he laughs and crying when he cries. 'I no longer live,' writes St Paul to the Galatians (2.20), 'but Christ lives in me.' The early Christians believed that in their conversion they had followed Christ in becoming sons of God. Baptism was therefore regarded as a symbol of death to their own lives and a rebirth into a new life in Christ. They were told that they had, quite literally, become *christoi* ('Christs'), and the Eastern Orthodox Church still refers to us becoming 'deified' like Christ in our lives. In other words, what Christ's physical presence did for the world 2,000 years ago, we now do for today's world. In Tom Waits' 2006 song 'Road to Peace', the renowned singer-songwriter describes the troubles of the Middle East and asks why God does not intervene to put an end to the bloodshed. He comes to the incarnational conclusion that for things to change, 'God himself he needs all of our help'. After all, we are God's hands, feet, mouth and heart on earth.

If the incarnation never came to an end, then, the power that God has in this world now comes principally through his followers. God is still very much in flesh around us today. Ronald Rolheiser tells the story of a four-year-old child who, waking up in the middle of the night, finds herself fearful of the darkness and scared about the possibility of ghosts and monsters hiding in the dark. She runs through to her parents' bedroom and tells them of her fears. Her mother comforts her by reassuring her that she is safe, as God is in her bedroom with her. The small child replies, 'I know that God is there, but I need someone in my room who has some skin.' The incarnation reassures us, as people who rely so much on our senses, that God still, quite literally, 'has some skin' and that he is here on earth in the shape of his followers. 'God still has skin, human skin,' writes Rolheiser, 'and he physically walks on this earth just as Jesus did.'

In the New Testament, the continuing presence of Christ in today's world is closely related to the expression the 'body of Christ'. The phrase is used to refer not just to the historical person of Jesus himself and to the bread and wine of the communion service, but to the body of believers on earth. On the road to Damascus, when confronted with a bright light and a voice from the heavens, Paul asks who is speaking to him. 'I am Jesus,' comes the answer, 'whom you are persecuting.' Jesus identifies himself with the body of believers that Paul is persecuting. Jesus and his followers are one and the same. Christians, then, are themselves a 'real presence' of Christ on earth. It is clear from Paul's subsequent letters that we do not replace Christ's body. We do not even represent Christ's body. Rather, we quite literally *are* Christ's body. There is a famous story about a priest who, when he celebrated Eucharist, would not bow to the host in front of him, but would turn round and bow to the congregation. That, after all, was where the physical real presence of Jesus was found.

The same conclusion was reached by the Cistercian priest Charles de Foucauld, who dedicated his life to the non-Christian people of Algeria. In the 1890s, de Foucauld settled in Nazareth, believing that to truly imitate Christ's life he should reside in the same place that Jesus did. After three years in Palestine, however, he concluded that his literal presence in Nazareth was unnecessary, as wherever we are we carry Christ with us. Nazareth, he wrote, 'is everywhere'. He subsequently devoted himself to standing alongside the poor and oppressed in North Africa, demanding nothing from those he helped. This, he believed, is what Jesus would have done. 'I should carry on in myself the life of Jesus,' he wrote in his journal, 'think his thoughts, repeat his words and his actions; may it be he that lives in me.' He even prophetically suggested that to follow Christ crucified we must be prepared for even the very worst consequences. 'I must lead the life of the cross,' he wrote, a few years before local rebels came to his hermitage and shot and killed him.

For most of us, 'taking up our cross' (Luke 9.23) will not, of course, mean a literal martyrdom. Still, an awareness that Christ is present in us will certainly make demands on us. St Paul's description of us as the 'body of Christ' in 1 Corinthians 12 tells us more about what it means to be incarnational. First, each part of the body is recognized as important. After all, in the analogy of the body, we are reminded that we ourselves need even the seemingly insignificant parts of our bodies. Second, all parts of the body are related to the head of the body. In the body of Christ this is Jesus himself, and as a result of our bond with him we are all automatically in a relationship with one another. So being a Christian is not about living an individual life of prayer, biblical study or contemplation, however important those things may be. Rather, being a Christian is living out that sense of community and fostering compassionate relationships with others. Thus we bear each other's burdens and stand alongside each other in love. There is, therefore, no such thing as 'your' problem and 'my' problem in the body of Christ. The whole body suffers if even one person is sick, lonely, depressed or hungry. As such, the incarnation directly opposes Thomas Hobbes' claim that being at war with ourselves and with each other is the 'natural' state of humankind. Our natural state is rather an interconnected harmony with God, with each other and with the world around us. By moving towards that harmony, we move towards our reason for being and find our purpose in life.

Christ in us – living as Christ

Being a part of the 'body of Christ' certainly demands from us a practical response that reaches out far beyond our weekly religious observances. Søren Kierkegaard, the nineteenth-century Danish philosopher, pointed out that while many people admire Christ, admiring him is not the same as following him. Similarly, simply worshipping him is not the same as following him. As Christians, so often our Sunday worship either makes Jesus a divine 'friend' to accompany us on our journeys or, worse, it lifts Christ so high that he lies beyond our reach for the rest of the week. Either way, we run the risk of separating the Word from the flesh. The principal goal of the Christian faith, after all, is not just to worship Christ, and goes beyond simply following Christ. Rather, we should aim to live 'in Christ', as we become Christ to others and take him out to our neighbours. 'For to me, to live is Christ,' writes St Paul to the Philippians (1.21).

Incarnationalism, then, means far more than simply imitating Christ in our lives. A monkey may well be able to blow into a clarinet, but this does not make it a talented musician. Imitating Christ does not mean just copying his external behaviour. We actually have to become Christ. We have to be what Christ was – not by merely imitating the love he showed us, but by actually becoming that love. In his letter to the Philippians, Paul exhorts his readers to take on the mind of Christ (Philippians 2.5). While the Greek word here (*phronesis*) is often translated 'mind', it can also mean 'attitude' or 'mindset'.

This is true incarnation, where Christ lives through us, through our attitudes and through our mindsets. In the same section of Philippians, Paul describes Christ emptying himself (*kenosis*) by taking the form of a human being and becoming a servant to others. Thus we are challenged to demonstrate our *phronesis* with our own *kenosis*. We are called to have the mind of Christ (*phronesis*) that is expressed in a self-emptying servanthood to others (*kenosis*). Like Christ, we need to become servants, emptying ourselves of prestige and power and compassionately identifying ourselves with people who are facing pain and suffering. As South African minister Xola Skosana asserted, as he embarked on a 30-day hunger strike to highlight institutionalized poverty in South Africa, 'the Church needs to step in and say "we don't have all the answers, but our call is to walk alongside people, our call is to hold somebody's hand, our call is to give people hope".' Words are often meaningless to a post-modern world, yet concrete acts of compassion, love and justice are as valued as they have always been. 'You are a letter from Christ,' Paul wrote to the church of Corinth (2 Corinthians 3.3), 'written not with ink but with the Spirit of the living God.'

Countless instances could be taken from history showing how certain people down the ages have lived out Christ in a practical way in the face of an often hostile world. Clarence Jordan was a Baptist biblical scholar who was deeply disturbed by the racial and economic injustice in the US Deep South in the 1940s. He confronted the hostile segregation of his community head on, by establishing an interracial Christian farming community in Georgia. He named his experiment Koinonia, from the Greek word meaning communion or fellowship – the same word is used in the book of Acts to refer to the early Jerusalem church, whose members shared all their belongings and resources. Koinonia's very presence challenged the deep-seated racism and materialism of the society in which it was based, as it championed equality, ecological stewardship and common ownership. By the 1950s, Koinonia had become the target of an economic boycott and a campaign of violence and terror, including several bombing attacks on the buildings. An appeal to the US President, Dwight Eisenhower, was unsuccessful; he refused to intervene and instead forwarded the case to the local governor, who was a staunch supporter of racial segregation and persecuted the community even further. In 1969 Jordan died of a heart attack, and even in death continued to be reviled by his enemies, with the coroner refusing to visit the farm to deal with Jordan's body.

Clarence Jordan's life certainly embodied what 'becoming' Christ involves. It is an obligation to live out the gospel, whatever the cost. 'Faith is not belief in spite of the evidence,' he wrote, 'but a life in scorn of the consequences.' He particularly advocated Christ's Sermon on the Mount as the blueprint for what it means for faith in action. Still, he claimed that these three chapters in Matthew's Gospel (5–7) had barely been lived out by Christ's followers over 2,000 years. The sermon, he maintained, was 'a mighty gushing stream from which we've only taken one or two drops'. Yet when we become Christ and live out his teaching of love and compassion, a whole new divine nature is formed in us. The Father transmits his own nature to his children and we break completely with our former Master – whether that master was materialism or prejudice or hatred. As such, we become like God, which is why the Sermon on the Mount calls us 'children of God'. According to Jordan, we don't take the Lord's name in vain with our lips, but rather with our lives, as we call ourselves Christians yet do not become Christ. In this sense, it is not those outside the Church that take the Lord's name in vain – they have never attributed themselves with the name to be able to do so. Rather, it is Christians who take the Lord's name in vain by living a life totally unchanged by God's grace.

By becoming Christ, then, it is imperative that our lives demonstrably change. We are in fact discarding the 'I' in us by making such a move. In Flannery O'Connor's novel *The*

Violent Bear It Away, a stranger suggests to young Tarwater that everyone has a simple choice in life. This choice is an 'either/or' that we all have to face. Tarwater presumes that this must be a choice between Jesus and the devil. 'No, no, no,' the stranger answers, 'it ain't Jesus or the devil. It's Jesus or you.' This is *Gelassenheit*, a concept referred to by German mystics in the Middle Ages. Today the term *Gelassenheit* has come to refer to 'serenity' or 'self-composure', but in medieval Germany it denoted the idea of 'I-lessness'. In other words, it referred to the discarding of our ego and our worldly attachments in order to embrace the 'Christ' in us. The fourteenth-century contemplative Henry Suso wrote of our complete surrender to God's will. We therefore relegate all those things that we are told by our society we should value – property, health, education, career, comfort, sexuality, success and achievements. Instead, everything becomes secondary to the Christ in us.

The frequent Christian contemplative commands of 'turning away from the world' and 'denying the world' should be seen in this context. To 'deny the world' refers to a conscious act on our part of rejecting our selfish and self-centred desires. The use of the word 'world' here represents a selfish desire for our own personal happiness over and above the needs and rights of others. Through turning away from the 'world' and towards Christ, who embodies compassion and love, we are freed to truly love both those made in his image and in his creation. So by embracing the sharp delineation between God and the world we are in no way denying human beings or the rest of creation. Rather, this leads us to care more about the world around us, as we allow our love for the world to flow out of the rejection of self-centredness.

Christ in others – our suffering neighbours

Alongside our recognition of the Christ in ourselves, the other profound implication that the incarnation brings to our theology

53

and to our everyday lives is that we are also led to recognize the Christ in others. The incarnation, then, helps us to move away from the traditional overemphasis on the 'Christ up above' and towards a recognition of the 'Christ down below', as we see him in the poor, weak and suffering creatures of the world. Again, this is wholly consistent with Scripture, with Jesus himself (in Matthew 25.31–46) describing how he will continue to be in human form after his death and resurrection. Thus, when we respond to the needs of others we are responding to Christ's own needs, and when we ignore their needs we are ignoring him. 'Truly I tell you,' asserts Matthew 25.40, 'whatever you did for one of the least of these brothers and sisters of mine, you did for me.' Our lives must be a process of recognizing Christ in the other, and especially the other who is enduring suffering or difficulty.

Charles de Foucauld viewed his whole ministry as a para-doxical process of taking Christ to people he already regarded as Christ. His house in Algeria became a place where the locals knew that they were welcome at any time. However poor they were, or however sick they were, they would be invited in with joy and then loved and cherished by de Foucauld and his friends. These people were to him, quite literally, 'the greatest treasure of all, Jesus himself'. Furthermore, he did not exclude anybody from his incarnational vision, as he considered that all humans were images of Christ and thus blessed members of his body. 'We are all children of God,' he wrote in his journal. 'We must therefore see the beloved children of God in all people, and not just in the good, not just in the Christians, not just in the Saints, but in all the people.'

Yet replacing the 'Christ up above' with this 'Christ down below' seems to run counter to today's instincts. Our society, after all, is almost obsessed with the concept of power. We even refer to our political parties as being 'in power' when they hold a majority in parliament, although in reality they are 'in service' to the people of the country. This obsession with power has long infected our faith, from the time of the conversion of Constantine through to the crusades in the Middle Ages and, more recently, in the colonial British Empire. Christ, however, is certainly not simply someone powerful and mighty to be worshipped. 'The mania for adoring or worshipping power,' writes Dorothee Soelle, 'is not cured by writing "Jesus" on one's banners instead of Hitler or Mussolini.' Martin Luther had earlier urged his readers to 'draw Christ into our flesh'. In other words, we must not spiritualize him into something powerful and ethereal, rather we must bring him into even the most mundane aspects of our everyday lives. We can certainly learn much from contemporary Latin American devotion, which is increasingly championing Christ the Companion (*companero cristo*) over Christ the King (*cristo rey*).

In practice, though, so many Christians seem to be uncomfortable with such an incarnational theology. 'Today I will start with a three-part sermon on: Jesus was HIV-positive,' Xola Skosana began a service in his church in Cape Town in September 2010. His words were recounted in his local press, and within days the sermon had been reported by the BBC and Sky News, and social network sites were soon buzzing with discussion as to the 'appropriateness' of such a claim. Having lost two of his sisters to Aids, Skosana explained his statement by pointing to Isaiah 53, where the suffering servant takes upon himself the infirmities and the pains of humankind. 'Wherever you open the scriptures,' he concluded, 'Jesus puts himself in the shoes of people who experience brokenness.' The level of misunderstanding that ensued among some sections of Christians revealed a faith that is not only more concerned with judgementalism than compassion, but also increasingly divorced from the biblical concept of incarnationalism. The *Daily Mail* reported that another South African minister, Mike Bele, had commented that he believed 'no anointed leader with a sound mind about the scriptures and the role of Christ in our lives would deliberately drag the name of Christ to the ground'. Yet a truly incarnational faith should be doing exactly that – bringing Christ down to the mud and the blood of this often cruel world. Thus a truly incarnational faith must recognize Christ in even the most upsetting images of our broken world. Christ's own suffering is surely worthless and pointless unless it can teach us something about even the most disturbing suffering of countless nameless people in today's world. As Dorothee Soelle puts it, 'It is Christ who screams in psychosis and tears his face with his nails before they put him in a straitjacket and quieten him down with injections.'

Christ in others – our groaning world

In the past, the consequence of the incarnation, like the rest of theology, has been largely related to humankind. Yet on Golgotha Jesus did not just represent humanity. Rather, the entire created order was tortured on the cross, while the resurrection promises redemption for the whole cosmos. Centuries of Platonic dualism have led us subconsciously to believe that matter is detrimental to our relationship with God. Instead, we should recognize that Christ lives and works in the world, and is present in every created thing. 'The beginning and end of all God's work is embodiment,' wrote Elisabeth Moltmann-Wendel. In other words, our experience of God is embodied in the material universe – in humankind, in the structures of society and in every aspect of nature. Such a realization should inspire us to a global compassion and love that transcends nations, race, cultures and even species. 'And when people look at creation with sympathy, with trust, then they will see the Lord,' asserted Hildegard of Bingen. 'It is God which humankind is then able to recognize in every living thing.'

The Christ of the New Testament was certainly very much part and parcel of the natural order around him. He was concerned with oppression, illness and disability, but the prologue of John's Gospel shows that Christ transcends mere human issues. God is, after all, concerned with the entire cosmos, which the *logos* continually creates and sustains. Thus it is only natural that Jesus' parables are full of references to nature and that his miracles included his direct interaction with the natural world, as he calmed storms and walked on water. St Paul himself had no problem with recognizing Jesus as the centre of the cosmos: he maintains that the whole of the created order is involved in Christ's salvation (Colossians 1.17, 20), as it groans 'as in the pains of childbirth' (Romans 8.22) for the day of redemption, when all things will be gathered up into him (Ephesians 1.10).

In light of this, the concept of the body of Christ takes on another important element, as the whole cosmos, not just the body of believers, can be seen to be part of this body. 'Christ, through his incarnation,' wrote Teilhard de Chardin, 'is internal to the world, rooted in the world, even in the very heart of the tiniest atom.' The entire universe, then, is the body of Christ and so our experiences of creation are as intimate to Christ as our bodies are to us. This is radical incarnationalism, where we recognize that Christ is in everything, not merely in everyone. Sometimes we may well have to make certain choices between different forms of life, but we must always start with an attitude of respect for all life in the body of Christ. 'If you're not interested in the plant world, the animal world, the physical world,' writes Richard Rohr, 'you haven't discovered the great Christ yet; your Christ is too small.'

This has particular relevance to us in the twenty-first century, as we face unprecedented threats to the environment around us. As we watched a film about global warming, I explained to my small daughter that the environment was slowly being destroyed and that 'the world is poorly'. Her expression was one of horror. 'Really?' she exclaimed. 'But surely that means that God is poorly!' While the transcendent is certainly more than the sum of his creation, there is still something profoundly true about that sentiment. If we recognize that the incarnation reaches out beyond humanity alone and that Christ is truly present in the living world around us, then we surely should be inspired to make bolder moves towards healing the brokenness of our fragile world. Pollution and deforestation are leading to changes in the world's atmosphere that are threatening all manner of life on dry land and in the sea, while many farmed animals are still subject to cruelty, yet most of us are indifferent to their living conditions and their fate. Some Christians tend to worry more about doctrinal theology and personal morality than about the treatment of God's awe-inspiring world and his precious creatures.

We need to follow the Cosmic Christ, so we can begin to liberate our suffering world. It is only through radical incarnationalism that we can subvert the medieval world-view, with its hierarchy of status and value, descending in decreasing order of perfection – heavenly beings at the top, then humanity, then animals and plantlife, and finally inanimate minerals at the bottom. The Latin phrase for this concept was *scala naturae*, literally meaning 'ladder' or 'stairway of nature'. It was believed that the strict hierarchical structure had been decreed by God himself, who as the perfect being sits in his glory at the top. Today's predominant world-view likewise has a hierarchical structure, the medieval ladder having been supplanted by a capitalist hierarchy of status and value. Wealth, success and achievement reside at the pinnacle of this new hierarchy, with poverty, failure and anonymity propping up its base. It is the duty of our faith to give to the world an alternative to both the medieval and the capitalist hierarchies. In fact, we need to discard any concept of hierarchy and embrace a new circle of creation, with all living beings regarded as loved and important. Christ himself will stand as the very heartbeat that drives this circle, as he, embodied in the world, stands alongside the suffering and the oppressed, both human and non-human, working to redeem them and offer them new life and new hope.

5

Radical compassion

————•◆•————

'Don't the Bible say we must love everybody?' 'Oh, the Bible!
To be sure, it says a great many things; but, then, nobody ever
thinks of doing them.'
                          Harriet Beecher Stowe, Uncle Tom's Cabin

The whole idea of compassion is based on a keen awareness
of the interdependence of all these living beings, which are all
part of one another and all involved in one another.
                Thomas Merton, written two hours before his death

One of the most persistent legends in the Christian tradition
is that of the quest for the Holy Grail, the chalice used by Jesus
for his last supper. A French poet of the late twelfth century,
Chrétien de Troyes, was the first to attempt a systematic retelling of the Holy Grail story, but his work was left unfinished.
The earliest complete recounting of the legend is a medieval
German text written by a Bavarian knight named Wolfram Von
Eschenbach and completed around the year 1200. His work,
entitled *Parzival*, served to inspire numerous later versions of
the story, from Sir Walter Scott and Richard Wagner to Monty
Python and *The Da Vinci Code*. In *Parzival*, the Holy Grail is
owned by the Fisher King, and it is this mysterious object that
keeps him alive, even when he is gravely wounded in his castle.
For him to receive complete healing, however, a knight has to
visit him and ask the 'correct' question. At one point, Parzival
turns up at the castle, but as a young, inexperienced knight he
fails to say the right thing and the King continues to suffer. But
at the end of the epic poem Parzival finally solves the riddle

and works out the question – he simply asks compassionately about the older man's health. His concern and kindness serve not only to heal the Fisher King but also to make Parzival the new Lord of the Holy Grail. For Eschenbach, then, compassion *is* the Holy Grail, as it is the one thing that God desires us to put into action, and it is what will bring us the ultimate reward. In practice, however, most of us fail to recognize 'the correct question', the question of love and compassion, and so we live a life that is ultimately unfulfilled.

Misplaced emphasis

In the modern-day quest for the Holy Grail of compassion, it is a sad irony that our faith has too often become a stumbling block rather than an encouraging inspiration. On Morrissey's critically acclaimed 2004 album *You are the Quarry*, the one-time lead singer of 1980s iconographic pop group The Smiths announces he has finally found it in himself 'to forgive Jesus', who has caused him to have guilt, hang-ups and low self-esteem in many areas of his life. He finishes the song by screaming repetitively at Jesus – 'Do you hate me? Do you hate me?' It is certainly an unhappy fact of twenty-first-century life that while faith should offer unconditional love, hope and liberating forgiveness, it is regarded by many as intolerant, guilt-inducing and judgemental. Instead of being a source of forgiveness, the Christian faith is deemed to need forgiveness itself.

A friend of mine recounts with sadness and horror experiences from her schooling in a church school: in particular, one daily event that had a profoundly negative effect on her. Each morning she would be given two felt-tip pens and a blank sheet of paper. With a red pen she had to draw a large heart on the paper. She would then be instructed to carry the paper and a black pen around with her during the day, and each time she did 'something wrong' or had a 'bad thought' she had to draw a patch of black inside the heart. She recalls her feelings of guilt and worthlessness at the end of each day when she would look at the completely blackened image of her heart. It is little surprise that she forsook her faith in her teens. While church schools now present faith in far more loving and uplifting ways to our children, in many ways the damage has already been done; our ancestors in Christ have bequeathed us a generation of young people who regard faith as something that oppresses rather than gives life.

This *status quo* has, in the main, resulted from a static and myopic understanding of the doctrine of the Fall, preoccupied with our sinfulness in front of a perfect God. Recently I was invited to speak to a Christian postgraduate student group on the question 'What is it to be human?' When the organizers discovered that our sinful and corrupt nature was not going to be integral to my paper, the invitation was rescinded. As Christians, an emphasis on our estrangement from God, which underlies both individual and structural sin, is certainly important, but a theology that obsesses about depravity leads merely to guilt, self-loathing and even hatred. A healthier point of departure for our Christian world-view is the fact that we have been created in the 'image of God'. Our creation came before our Fall, and while the doctrine of original sin still has much to teach us with regard to our brokenness in relation to both God and our neighbour, our faith must never be blinded from the essential goodness of life. God himself, after all, emphasized in Genesis 1 that each part of creation is 'good' and the totality of creation is 'very good'. 'It is from the abundance of your goodness that your creation exists,' wrote Augustine at the end of his *Confessions*; 'all things have been made very good by you, the one supreme Good.'

As it stands, however, the Christian message has become distorted; an overemphasis on the Fall and our innate wickedness has led to the concept of compassion becoming an afterthought in some Christian circles. 'I've been in politics long enough to expect criticism and hostility,' Bill Clinton is reported to have told a group of journalists during his presidency, 'but I was unprepared for the hatred I get from Christians. Why do Christians hate so much?' In fact, numerous psychological and sociological studies have concluded that in today's world people of faith have no more inclination towards compassion than do agnostics or atheists. Psychologist William Eckhardt even claims that of those who are compassionate in the Western world, theists 'are in the minority'. In light of the centrality of compassion both in Scripture and in theology, this fact should shame and embarrass those of us who are Christian. It is astounding that the compassion that is so central to the life of Christ himself is not reflected in the lives of his followers today. In another study, James A. Christensen wrote, 'People who regularly attend church exhibit no greater social compassion than those who do not attend.'

God as compassion

The Genesis description of the creation of man and woman should be viewed as far more than a mere comment about marriage. In fact, it teaches us something profound about all of us and our relationships with each other. We are created to be in communion and to be gifts to one another. According to Jewish Midrash, creation itself came out of God's desire to share his compassion, and so it is our duty to take that compassion as a gift to everyone and everything we encounter. Thus our lives should be ones of self-giving love – to our families, to our friends and colleagues, to our communities, to our society, and to the natural world around us. In doing so, we reflect the essential being of the Trinity, which is a communion of mutual love. Compassion is, after all, not merely one of God's attributes. In the book of Exodus (34.6) we are told, on Mount Sinai, that both God's actual name and his fundamental being are related to compassion. 'You may call God goodness; you may call God love,' wrote Meister Eckhart in the thirteenth century, 'but the best name for God is Compassion.'

By accepting that God himself is compassion, we ourselves are drawn to partake in the *imitatio dei*, the imitation of God, when we carry out an act of compassion. This, according to the prophet Hosea (6.6), is more important than any worship or liturgy. While a number of words in the Old Testament can be, and often are, translated as 'compassion', the most frequent is the word *rachamim*. 'The LORD Almighty said: "Administer true justice; show mercy and compassion [*rachamim*] to one another"' (Zechariah 7.9). The word is related to the Hebrew term for womb, *rechem*, intimating that our compassion for those around us should reflect intimate familial bonds. In other words, we should treat others as if they had shared the same womb as we did, as if they were our own flesh and blood. Thus the archetype for compassion is fraternal, as we view all as our brothers and sisters, and treat them accordingly.

While the Old Testament presents God as compassion and urges us to imitate him in our everyday lives, the New Testament goes a step further, by giving us a tangible, living example of God as compassion and providing a blueprint for a radical model of compassion in our own lives. The person Jesus embodies the very heart of compassion. Christ's love is a love that empties itself of status, power or privilege and takes on the form of a servant to others. As such, compassion is central to the incarnation. Our God is a compassionate God precisely because he chooses to be 'God with us' – standing alongside us in our brokenness. Likewise, when we choose to be fully present to another, whatever hardships they are facing, we make a similar incarnational choice. The ultimate inspiration for us to practise this radical compassion is the cross itself. Our instinctive empathy for Christ on the cross challenges our hearts to take that compassion to others who are suffering. As the medieval theologian Peter Abelard put it, through Christ's sacrifice 'we are thus joined through his grace to him and our neighbour by an unbreakable bond of love'.

Referring directly to compassion, the New Testament in fact uses two different Greek words. The first word is *eleeo*, which is primarily used by those who appeal to Jesus for healing. The second word, *splanchnizomai*, expresses a deeper and more passionate form of compassion. In modern parlance it could literally be translated 'to be moved in one's guts', and is used for Jesus' own reaction to those who are pleading for healing. Jesus, therefore, responds to those who plea for basic compassion (*eleeo*) with a compassion that is intimate and intense (*splanchnizomai*). The pain and suffering of others engenders not merely superficial sympathy in Jesus, but rather affects him in the core of his being. Jesus was compassion incarnate – compassion made flesh – and it is this deep-seated compassion that leads him to do something about the suffering with which he is confronted. It might be said, then, that it is not necessarily the physical healing itself that reveals God in Jesus' miracles, but that God is revealed in the compassion that leads to the cure. 'The mystery of God's love is not that our pain is taken away,' wrote Henri Nouwen, 'but that God first wants to share the pain with us.'

Philip Pullman's apocryphal retelling of Jesus' life, *The Good Man Jesus and the Scoundrel Christ*, vividly expresses the scandal of such radical compassion. Jesus is presented as having a twin brother, simply called 'Christ', who follows him around the Palestinian countryside, interpreting his teachings and his actions. He is particularly shocked at Jesus' teaching about God's compassion and grace. The parables Jesus tells (the good Samaritan, the prodigal son, the lost sheep, the great feast, and so on) describe a universal love that is arbitrary and undeserved, almost like a lottery, and the twin brother believes that this is simply a 'horrible' way of viewing love. Furthermore, Jesus' lifestyle reflects this 'unfair' concept of love. He mixes with undesirables like tax collectors and prostitutes, he claims to be ushering in a time of compassion by announcing the coming kingdom of God, and he condemns much of what was considered as virtue at the time. In Pullman's tale, the whole situation seriously disturbs the scoundrel 'Christ', and so he completely rejects his twin brother as naive and delusional. Yet it is this very attitude that is the crux of both the teachings and the actions of Jesus – an uncompromising, self-giving, unconditional compassion that transcends religious, political or ethnic differences. 'What is needed is a radicalism that leads beyond both the right and left,' writes Jim Wallis, the Christian political activist who serves as spiritual advisor to Barack Obama, 'that radicalism that can be found in the gospel which is neither liberal nor conservative but fully compassionate.'

Radical compassion in practice

Compassion is at the very heart of the Christian gospel. God is love, and compassion is that love in action in our lives. Thus, when we are compassionate, we fully connect with God, the truly compassionate one. Mechthild of Magdeburg, the medieval contemplative, suggested that compassion is the process by which we become more like the divine. Just as evangelism, in the theological concept of *missio dei*, is not rooted in our own efforts but in our alignment with God's mission, so compassion is an active decision to enter into the ongoing work of the Creator God himself. We cannot achieve compassion on our own, but rather we open ourselves to the divine, who continually wills compassion on his creation. In other words, we open our hearts to, and become part and parcel of, the *compassio dei*. 'God created a reminder, an image – humanity is a reminder of God,' wrote Rabbi Abraham J. Heschel shortly before his death. 'As God is compassionate, let humanity be compassionate.'

Being compassionate, therefore, means recognizing the image of God in each and every person. In other words, we must work to become aware of our own backgrounds, prejudices and conditioning, so that we view people as they truly are, rather than as we imagine them to be. By doing so, we acknowledge that all are fully loved by God and thus we cannot fail to be moved by their suffering. After all, compassion is far more than observing that another person is suffering and thereby sympathizing with them. Rather, it is an active undertaking of entering and sharing the suffering of the other person. 'Remember those in prison as if you were together with them in prison,' notes the letter to the Hebrews (13.3), 'those who are ill-treated as if you yourselves were suffering.' There is even scientific evidence to suggest that such compassion is not so alien to what Richard Dawkins describes as our 'ruthlessly selfish' genes. Recent research shows that we do, quite literally, feel for other people when we see them suffering. Our 'mirror neurons', located at the front of our brains, light up on the neurologist's computer screen when we are shown distressing images of suffering. As a result, we truly do feel the pain of another by watching them experience it.

When she was a child, the French philosopher Simone Weil is said to have been helping her parents move house when she noticed that her brother was struggling with a far heavier box than hers. 'Feeling' the struggle that her poor brother was undergoing, she put her own load on the floor, sat on it, and refused to help any further until she was given a similarly heavy box! In fact, this sense of compassion was reflected throughout her life, which itself was cut short in 1943 when she was only 34, partly as a result of an act of solidarity for her suffering compatriots. Although she was already very ill with tuberculosis, she rationed her food intake to what she believed the Jews in occupied France were being allowed to eat. 'As for her death,' wrote her biographer Richard Rees, 'whatever explanation one may give of it will amount in the end to saying that she died of love.'

Although such an extreme empathy as was felt by Simone Weil towards the world is unusual, radical compassion is always paradoxical, as the very process of joining someone in their suffering so as to help alleviate that suffering seems illogical. After all, it goes completely against our logic to be freed by someone who is imprisoned or to get directions from someone who is lost. Yet we cannot allow logic to limit *kenosis*, the self-sacrificial emptying of ourselves for others. Like Christ, we become slaves, so that we can liberate our fellow slaves. As Karl Barth put it, Jesus moves from 'the heights to the depth, from victory to defeat, from riches to poverty, from triumph to suffering, from life to death', bringing to others those very things that he had moved away from himself.

As Christians, then, compassion should be at the very centre of our lives, rather than at the periphery. We should be championing it to our children and teaching it in our schools above the desire for success and achievement. Albert Schweitzer argued that children have a basic capacity for compassion, which needs to be nurtured if it is to grow and thrive. Furthermore, once compassion is fostered in our children and in ourselves, we would more than likely see a snowball effect, as people 'pay it forward', as the film of that name put it. The more we give, the more others (and often ourselves) will receive in return. Individuals, communities and societies are thus enlivened and brought hope through this process. Like ripples on a pond, our compassion will have far-reaching effects on far more people than we realize. 'If money goes, money comes,' claimed Dr Aziz in E. M. Forster's *A Passage to India*, 'if money stays, death comes.' Our faith does not remain behind stained-glass windows, where its pious and sanctimonious character confirms itself as irrelevant and trivial. Rather, we give ourselves joyously in radical compassionate love for others, as we act, in the words of Etty Hillesum, 'as a balm for all wounds'.

Radical compassion as the meaning of life

At the very heart of radical compassion is an awareness of our mutuality and togetherness. If we truly hold to our close relationship with the rest of creation, then we cannot fail to be compassionate. The realization that we are part of a greater whole inspires us to stand alongside each other. 'They're luckiest who know they're not unique,' writes the poet Adrienne Rich. We need, then, to transcend our self-centredness and desire the best for others. Love does not will our own good through the other, claimed Thomas Aquinas, but it simply wills the good of the other. By living out love in this way, we are liberated from the Cartesian emphasis on the individual that humankind has been allied to for far too long. For most of us, the idea that we are interrelated and interdependent seems alien. In reality, though, we are all utterly dependent on others throughout our lives, particularly when we are young and in our final years. Newborn animals will quickly utilize their instincts to find food, and so their parents are not required for long. Human babies, on the other hand, are completely reliant on others for many months and years. In a way, compassion is simply an extension of the care that we all receive from the moment we are born and continue to receive at other times during our lives.

Despite our complete reliance on others, we seem to relate instinctively to our separateness rather than to our inter-connectedness. Thus our faith demands that we sacrifice our old, selfish, separate selves and be reborn as more caring, compassionate souls. In chapter 8 of his letter to the Romans, Paul exhorts us to die to our sinful self. This is our non-compassionate and self-centred self, which always thinks of ourselves in opposition to others. As a popular, humorous bumper-sticker petitions God: 'If you can't help me lose weight, Lord, then please make my friends gain weight.' Such an attitude is the polar opposite to compassion, and is related to what the Germans call *schadenfreude* – the pleasure at another person's pain. True compassion, instead, is centred on kinship, together-ness and a desire to stand alongside the other in all his or her experiences, whether painful or joyful. We are not made either to suffer or to celebrate alone, but rather for communion at both the highs and the lows of our life journeys. An old German proverb sums this up: 'A sorrow shared is a sorrow halved; a joy shared is a joy doubled.'

This discarding of our old self-centred ways and the embracing of a new way of compassionate living can certainly be regarded as the very purpose of our existence. Clarence Jordan points to the historical development in Scripture towards an unconditional way of love and compassion. First, we hear of the *unlimited retaliation* of some of Israel's neighbours in the ancient Near East, where revenge and retribution were carried out to the point of annihilation. Then the Old Testament introduces us to *limited retaliation*, as God demands that the Israelites restrain their reprisals to the exact amount of their injury. 'You are to take life for life,' asserts Exodus 21.23–25, 'eye for eye, tooth for tooth, hand for hand, foot for foot, burn for burn, wound for wound, bruise for bruise.' Subsequently the early Israelites began to prescribe *limited love*, where it was accepted that compassion is important, but must be limited to people who deserve our love and empathy. 'You have heard that it was said,' Jesus said, '"Love your neighbour and hate your enemy".' Finally, Jesus himself introduces us to the concept of *unlimited love*. Unlimited love is the very essence of radical compassion, and must, for us Christians, become the very basis of all our relationships – our relationships with other humans, whoever they are and whatever harm they have done to us, and with the world around us. Clarence Jordan concluded: 'To talk about unlimited retaliation is babyish; to speak of limited retaliation is childish; to advocate limited love is adolescent; to practise unlimited love is evidence of maturity.'

The two great commandments of Jesus – loving God and loving each other – are therefore brought together in this concept of unlimited compassion (cf. Galatians 5.14). It is as if two targets were placed together, one behind the other, so that when an arrow hits one, it also hits the other. 'Love of God and love of neighbour are two yet one, at the same time,' writes Japanese theologian Kazoh Kitamori; 'because God is immanent in our neighbour, love of neighbour becomes love of God.' When we practise compassion we are thus making a statement about God, as well as about his creation. This can be done in very practical ways that all of us, whatever our circumstances, can undertake. We can live out compassion to the people around us – our families, our friends, our work colleagues, even strangers with whom we come into contact. We can proactively place ourselves in situations where people are suffering or struggling – through charities, churches, hospices or hospitals. We can extend our unlimited love to the wider world – either by joining movements for social or environmental change or by undertaking small acts of compassion for our pets, our gardens, or our towns and cities. In all these things, we become truly present to all life, standing alongside everything that suffers and offering Christ to the world with open arms and open hearts.

The challenge of radical compassion

Despite the clear biblical imperative towards a radical compassion, living out that ideal in our everyday lives is a continual challenge. Our culture, after all, is much more inclined towards 'pity' or 'charity' than compassion. The recent proliferation of charitable giving, aided by television (with the resounding success of telethons such as Children in Need, Comic Relief and Sports Relief) and the internet (the Just Giving website, for example, making charitable donations so simple), is certainly commendable. Charity, however, only goes so far and often serves to distance ourselves from those we aim to help. While responding to the basic human needs of the so-called less fortunate is necessary and right, charity still upholds a system that consolidates an 'us' and 'them' world-view, as even the term 'less fortunate' implies. We need to move beyond mere charity to a fundamentally new way of viewing our neighbours and the world around us.

In the same way that charity can distance us from 'the other', pity also implies a separateness. The whole process of pitying places us in a position of power, superiority and strength, as we implicitly contrast ourselves with the weaknesses of the other person. Compassion, on the other hand, is rooted in solidarity, and in a recognition that we are all involved in journeys that will include many sorts of suffering at various times. Thus, when we stand alongside our brothers and sisters, we do so in the hope that compassion will be returned to us in our own hours of need. Even the words 'compassion' and 'pity' show their dissimilarities. 'Compassion' derives from the Latin words *cum* and *pati*, meaning 'to suffer with', and this contrasts markedly with 'pity', which has close links to the words 'piety' and 'pious'. When we pity we often act as if we know better than the other person, while compassion simply leads us to feel the suffering of another as if it were our own – we willingly enter the places of pain in people's lives.

In the Old Testament, Job's friends are initially inspired towards compassion, as they go to him with the aim of standing alongside and comforting their distraught friend. On arriving, they empathize with his lot by entering his suffering in a way typical of Israelite culture – by weeping, tearing their clothing and throwing dust on themselves. They then sit with Job in silence for a whole week, 'because they saw how great his suffering was' (Job 2.13). Their very presence was their compassion. If that had been the conclusion of the story, it might indeed be an ideal model of incarnational compassion, albeit one rooted in the cultural practices of the ancient Near East. Unfortunately, for the next 35 chapters these friends ruin their earlier work by offering empty, critical and patronizing opinions on Job's predicament. Too often we are drawn to offer advice or counsel when we see someone suffering. Compassion, however, simply calls us to be there for those in need. I have a small

71

box at home that is stuffed with scribbled notes and business cards that I have acquired since my diagnosis of a degenerative spinal condition, containing the names and phone numbers of osteopaths, physiotherapists, chiropractors, acupuncturists, and reiki specialists. They have been given to me by friends, colleagues, and even strangers on trains who notice that I have to get up and walk around the carriage at every opportunity. Certainly all these people had a real desire to bring relief to my pain and, as such, their gestures were kindly and loving. Yet too often many of us fail to recognize that mere kindness is not enough and those suffering need something very different from 'advice'. The aspiration to 'mend' or to 'cure' is clearly well-meaning, but the real need of people who are suffering is an incarnational and compassionate giving of time and attention.

The road of compassion, however, will rarely offer us a smooth path. The social activist Dorothy Day would often warn new young volunteers at her Catholic Worker House that their enthusiasm and drive would soon be challenged. 'There are two things you need to know about the poor,' she would tell them: 'they are ungrateful and they smell.' By being compassionate we engage in real life, and real life naturally involves risks and dangers, including ingratitude. Thus compassion will often ask of us a marked personal sacrifice. Standing alongside those who suffer is part of the costly discipleship championed by Dietrich Bonhoeffer. By its very nature, such discipleship makes demands on us, as we embrace the crucifixion by following the way of the cross. Yet compassion should never be masochistic. In his letter to the Philippians, St Paul continually relates compassionate service to both sacrifice and joy, reminding us that while compassion is not always easy, it still can be acted out with a sense of hope and joy.

While compassion may not be an easy process, Christians have to reject categorically the claim that it is a naive venture. Our contemporary society is suspicious of our faith's survival-of-the-weakest attitude, being far more devoted to the competitive and individualistic mindset. 'No healthy society should allow itself to see the world through the eyes of the unfortunate,' wrote the British journalist and broadcaster Peregrine Worsthorne. This may seem an extreme viewpoint, but many of us continue to maintain a safe distance from those who are facing difficulties. We may even make a concerted effort to change the subject when people open up to us with their problems, or offer to take them out to 'get their minds off their problems'. Rarely do we actively seek to suffer alongside our neighbours, and even more rarely do we follow Jesus' radical stance by showing compassion towards everybody, not just 'those who deserve it'.

In the six-time Oscar-nominated *Up in the Air* (2009), George Clooney plays a corporate downsizer, who informs workers of their impending redundancies and gives motivational speeches at conferences. In one of these talks, entitled 'What's in Your Backpack?', he extols the virtue of emptying our metaphorical bags of the burdensome 'things' in our lives. After clearing our backpack of possessions and material belongings, he then suggests emptying it also of people and relationships. These are, after all, the heaviest, most troublesome components in our lives. 'Can you feel the straps of your backpack cutting into your shoulders?' he asks the audience, 'all those negotiations, and arguments, and secrets, and compromises – you don't need to carry all that weight!' Finally he urges his listeners to discard their backpacks completely, so as to concentrate on being carefree and successful. He concludes that compassion, love and sacrifice are simply for the weak, unsuccessful failures in this life: 'Some animals are meant to carry each other, to live symbiotically for a lifetime – star-crossed lovers, monogamous swans. We are not those animals. The slower we move, the faster we die. We are not swans. We are sharks.'

While such an extreme view might be rare, our society does seem to value competition more than compassion, and many of us are unconsciously led to accept such a view. Being compassionate may be viewed as very worthy, but when it comes down to it modern wisdom teaches that it gets us nowhere in the cut and thrust of this world. In fact, more often than not, compassion is seen as naive and unrealistic, even among some people of faith. At a two-week colloquium I recently attended, the world-weary chairperson of our group, a retired Church of England clergyman, continually dismissed any suggestions of combating poverty, prejudice and oppression with self-sacrificial love and compassion. We were, according to him, being far too 'utopian' and 'idealistic'. Yet the kingdom of God is exactly that – an ideal, utopian vision. Its visionary and optimistic character does not make it any less desirable or pertinent. Jesus certainly did not advocate compassion on the basis of its practicality. In fact, as Clarence Jordan put it, 'folks who are determined enough to hold onto it usually wind up on a cross'. In the long run, however, once we recognize the interconnectedness of the world around us, God's kingdom has to be centred on unconditional, radical compassion, however idealistic and unrealistic that might seem to an unbelieving world. The kingdom is all about 'the relevance of the impossible ideal', as Reinhold Niebuhr put it, and each of us needs to radically regrasp and reclaim that wonderful compassionate ideal.

6

There but for the grace of God

I spent 10 years teaching in a prison . . . I realized that people in prison were like me. They could have been in my shoes, or I could have been in theirs. It's such a fine line sometimes.

Prison teacher to Kristin Scott Thomas in
I've Loved You So Long *(2010)*

It is worrisome that so much should be made to depend on the whims of fate, unless it is to make us more modest and less dogmatic in our claims.

Archbishop Desmond Tutu

Alexander Masters' award-winning book *Stuart: A Life Backwards* tells the true story of a homeless man living on the streets of Cambridge. The first few chapters present Stuart Shorter as an infamous character in the city – a violent, heroin-addicted alcoholic. For many years he had been in trouble with the police, for theft, drugs, GBH and much more. His sad situation was, it seems, entirely his own 'fault'. He was choosing to live a life of drugs, alcohol and violence. We are then, however, taken backwards through his life, and we soon realize that perhaps our judgements and prejudices need to be reassessed. At a very early age, Stuart Shorter had been diagnosed with muscular dystrophy, and was bullied horribly at school because of his contorted body. He was moved to a school for children with disabilities, but subsequently teased and bullied further on his housing estate for being in a 'special' school. At this same time, both his older brother and his babysitter began systematically sexually abusing him. Stuart was so traumatized that, without telling anyone the reason, he demanded to be put into care, in order to escape his abusers. But the government care home he was sent to was run by someone who would himself later be convicted of serious sexual child abuse. Stuart was one of hundreds of young boys regularly abused by this notorious paedophile. By the end of the book we are left asking ourselves whether, if we had been through the terrible experiences that Stuart Shorter had endured, we also would be living self-destructive lives. On 6 July 2002 Stuart Shorter, aged only 33, ended his short, tragic life by stepping in front of the 11.15 train from London to Kings Lynn.

Sadly, many people have similarly traumatic upbringings and backgrounds. 'We're not bad people – we just come from a bad place,' Carey Mulligan tells her brother Michael Fassbender in the BAFTA-nominated *Shame* (2011). Yet people are not open books. Situations and backgrounds are not clear for all to see, and so we tend to judge others directly on what we observe them doing, how they act, or on what others tell us about them. The love and compassion we offer may well be limited, and conditional on how others act towards us; showing grace is often seen either as naive or as a weakness. As someone was overheard to remark, after a meeting about the increasing schism in Anglicanism with the then Archbishop of Canterbury, 'The trouble with Rowan Williams is that he loves everybody.'

Yet Christ himself lived out a limitless love, shocking the religious authorities of the time by refusing to judge others by how they looked, what they did, or how they acted. He socialized with tax collectors and prostitutes, he spoke to Samaritans and gentiles, and he physically touched those who were regarded as unclean by first-century Jewish standards. Furthermore, in his parables the message was that God's kingdom is open to everyone, whatever their race, colour, nationality, class, education or wealth. 'Inside the kingdom there are no partitions,' John Dominic Crossan reflects on the parable of the wedding banquet. 'The ones who would erect them thereby declare themselves to be on the outside.'

Nature and nurture

While most of us will, thankfully, not have had as traumatic a start in life as Stuart Shorter, we are each from a unique and deeply influential life context. As such, we often find that our childhood and our early influences hold considerable control over us. The choices we make with regard to our lifestyles, our values and our relationships might not be as free as we might think. The profound effect of childhood bullying, for example, can be lifelong and pervasive. I have friends who were severely bullied at school, and they claim that even today their lives are being impacted by the cruelty they experienced. It still, for example, has a bearing on how they conduct relationships, how they form friendships and how they relate to their work colleagues. One friend is awoken regularly with nightmares of his school bullying. Yet even those of us who go through comparatively little trauma in our childhood are affected adversely, often without us knowing or realizing, by things said or done to us when we were children. On the other hand, positive and life-affirming events in our childhood also have lifelong effects. And it is not only our experiences as children and teenagers that have lasting consequences: psychologist Sue Gerhardt has shown that even influences during early infancy have an effect on our later life. Babies' nervous systems actually develop differently physiologically depending on the amount of love and care they receive. When a child is loved, the prefrontal cortex is stimulated, thus boosting confidence and empathy in adulthood. A lack of love, on the other hand, can lead to anxiety, anger and anti-social behaviour. Our everyday lives, then, are directly influenced by our infancy, despite our inability to even remember that formative period.

In reality, due to a mixture of our genetic make-up and our daily influences from a very early age, all of us could be taken apart and analysed piece by piece – you have your mother's eyes, your grandfather's nose, your father's anxiety, your brother's confidence, your childhood friend's sense of humour, and so on. We could even take, for example, particular sentences that we often say, and by going back far enough in our lives we could trace the origin of those phrases – our schooling, our family, a particular TV programme that we watched. Young children especially are like sponges when it comes to speech and mannerisms. My son picked up a habit of answering 'I don't know' with a drawled inflection – 'are dunno'. Within days his younger sister, only five years old, was answering 'are dunno' to every question we asked! And it is not only language that we pick up from those around us. We all consider ourselves to be free, but actually every thought we have, every emotion we feel, every attitude we express, and every belief we cherish, has its root in someone or something else, from our past or from our present. The 'I' in us, that which we value so very highly, is in many ways essentially a conglomeration of our genes, our conditioning, and our past and present experiences.

Scientists always take into account the environment within which an experiment occurs. In the same way, we are dealing with a false reality if we judge people without knowledge of their upbringing and, indeed, their genetic make-up. Such a complex and complete level of knowledge is impossible for us to ascertain, and so our temptation to judge others needs to be treated with extreme caution. It is almost impossible to condemn others completely when we face the reality that if we had their genes and a similar upbringing, there is a good chance that we would be acting in the same way. As the sixteenth-century English reformer John Bradford is purported to have exclaimed when he saw a group of prisoners being led to their execution: 'There but for the grace of God, goes John Bradford.'

We have, then, little or no control over the factors that determine our personalities, and numerous influences continue to assert a considerable hold on the decisions we make each day. No wonder Jesus was so critical of those 'hypocrites' he saw judging others. Many Christians continue to pride themselves on their moral values, but our ethical decisions might be very different if our upbringing or background were altered. Furthermore, even as we are now, our integrity might well slip away given certain circumstances; this has been shown to be the case when so-called 'Christian' countries have upheld and supported oppressive and hateful regimes.

This is not to say, of course, that God has not gifted us with control of our lives. We must certainly beware of the dangers of Determinism, a philosophical school of thought where the influence of both nature and nurture on our present conditions is taken to its furthest conclusion. 'You think we've got a choice?' asks Robert de Niro in *City by the Sea* (2002). 'No, we just pretend we've got a choice – it's more like a sentence.' Determinism maintains that human actions and decisions are not really our own choice, but are already determined. Yet, while we have to take our genes and our upbringing with utmost seriousness, Christians must also hold on to the fact that we are more than our biology and background. After all, there is so much in our make-up that hints that life is far more profound – not least the fact that we have an innate spirituality, which connects us with everything we come into contact with and helps us to appreciate the beauty and wonder of nature and art. Furthermore, God has placed in us a yearning for relationship, both with others and with him, which inspires us to reach out with arms of compassion to the world around us. We are not simply complex robots shackled by our backgrounds and our genes. Freedom of choice is not an illusion, as we must take responsibility for the decisions we make. We can hold to this truth without taking away from the fact that numerous unpredictable factors have a say in how someone turns out. In the 2002 science-fiction film *Minority Report*, Tom Cruise plays a police detective in a world where the future can be seen with absolute certainty, and so murderers can be arrested before the crime is committed. The ultimate message of the film, however, is that free will always has the potential to change the course of people's lives, even if it is at the very last moment. Our genes and upbringing may suggest that we are not completely free, but neither are we wholly in bondage to those factors, and our faith ensures that Christ liberates us from the utter dominance of the chains of nature and nurture.

It could have been me

Given a different background and childhood, then, our neighbours could actually be us and we them, and Christ's call for us to treat others as we would have them treat us is at the heart of this realization. This was brought home to me forcefully a few years ago, when I took a group of students to a former Nazi concentration camp so that they could ponder and reflect on this dreadful event in the recent history of Europe. Our visit was, understandably, a harrowing experience. At one point we all stood still outside one of the wooden huts in which the prisoners had slept, reduced to silence in the midst of our thoughts of the horrors the prisoners had faced – extreme hunger, freezing weather, physical pain and mental anguish. Then one student suddenly said: 'Imagine if we had been one of the guards here.' I could see the realization dawn on the faces of my students: yes, we could have been one of the prisoners, but equally we could have been one of the oppressors. We are so used to putting ourselves empathetically in the shoes of the oppressed that we forget that the oppressors are also human, just like you and me.

Rather than adopt the prevailing Cartesian individualistic world-view of 'I think therefore I am', Thich Nhat Hanh, the peace activist who was nominated for the Nobel Peace Prize by Martin Luther King, suggests that we should embrace a framework that asserts 'I am, therefore you are' and 'You are, therefore I am'. His prayer-poem 'Please Call Me by My True Names' was penned after he received a letter telling him about a young refugee girl who was raped by a Thai sea pirate while she attempted to cross the Gulf of Siam. The 12-year-old subsequently jumped into the ocean and drowned herself. In

the poem Hanh takes the concept of our mutual interconnectedness to its natural conclusion. If we hold to our oneness with
the universe around us, we are in some ways part and parcel
of all that we experience. In that sense, the poem asserts that
we actually *are* the mayfly, the bird who feasts on the mayfly,
the frog, the grass-snake who kills the frog, the starving child
in Uganda, the arms merchant selling arms to the Ugandans, the
young refugee girl, and even the rapist sea pirate. They are all of
us, and we are all of them. Hanh's poem touches upon a profound
truth which, while famously found in his own Buddhist beliefs,
is also reflected theistically in the Christian contemplative tradition: it is only when we recognize our own faces in both the
good and the bad of the world around us that the doors of our
hearts will be opened, and we will truly be able to welcome in
compassion and then share it with the world around us.

This recognition of our common humanity with even the most
notorious of criminals will help us guard ourselves from the
brutal desire to see offenders suffer. Forgiveness and mercy are
rare in today's world – the desire for revenge and retribution
is far more common. The Truth and Reconciliation Commission in South Africa was remarkable precisely because it is so
unusual for a political movement to be driven by forgiveness,
rather than punitive justice. It is of little surprise that faith
played a definitive part in the process, with each day beginning
with prayers led by the chairman of the meeting, Archbishop
Desmond Tutu, who wore his clerical collar and episcopal shirt
throughout the process. At the Commission, those who were
the oppressors during the apartheid regime came face to face
with the people they had oppressed and persecuted. In interviews that took place both during and after the process, Tutu
emphasized that both torturer and tortured were 'fellow children
of God' and thus were deserving of our love and compassion.
Not that he claimed that forgiveness was easy or cheap for those
who had been wronged. He pointed to how difficult we can
find it to apologize to or forgive our own husbands and wives

in the privacy of our own kitchens after an argument, let alone forgive those who have tortured and killed our friends and family. 'I'm afraid we are following a Lord and Master who, at the point when they were crucifying him in the most painful way, can say "pray for their forgiveness",' Tutu told an American television channel. 'We follow the one who says, "forgive one another as God in Christ forgives you". That is, for us, the paradigm – we may not always reach that ideal, but that is the standard.'

However heinous we regard the actions of others, our call should always be towards compassion. More often than not, however, those who have done terrible wrongs are dismissed in death as they were in life. The sickening actions of Myra Hindley, who was involved in the atrocious murder of five children on Saddleworth Moor in the 1960s, were clearly abhorrent, but the reactions after Hindley's death in 2002 reflect a society with little self-awareness of the fact that all of us have the capacity for the most horrendous evil as well as the greatest good. *The Sun* exclaimed that 'Myra the Devil' would never be forgiven, while the *Daily Mail* bemoaned the fact that she had a peaceful death; the front page headline of the *Daily Express* simply read 'Go to Hell, Myra'. The temptation is to demonize offenders and regard them as qualitatively 'different' from us and our loved ones. Reform, redemption and restoration are seen as naive and implausible, as we continue to separate and stigmatize those who act in ways that go against our moral codes. As *The Tablet* put it, referring to both Hindley and the Oklahoma bomber Timothy McVeigh:

> As a society we can point at Hindley and McVeigh, label them the Devil, and so separate ourselves entirely from them. They are not like us. They do not have the same human potential for good and bad. What they did is nothing to do with being human. *They* are not human.

Redemption, though, requires a recognition of similarity. By viewing such offenders as quantifiably different from us, we are led to believe that there can be no redemption for them. Yet for Christ himself nothing and no one was beyond redemption, as was reflected beautifully in the warm embrace given by Jesus to Judas Iscariot, after the betrayal, in the TV series *Jesus of Nazareth*. In the Gospel stories Christ's love, acceptance and compassion have no boundaries. So much so that the Eastern Orthodox tradition teaches that he not only died *for* us, he died *as* us. He became truly interconnected with us by becoming each and every one of us – murderers, rapists, terrorists – and on the cross he absorbed the pain of *all* our sins into himself. Kierkegaard wrote that as such he is 'eternally crucified', as he truly felt everything that humankind has been through, is going through, and will be going through in the future. As St Athanasius put it in the fourth century: 'He became what we are that we might become what He is.'

Labels

We distance ourselves even further from others by labelling people, often as soon as we meet them or before we get to know them. He is a man, she is a solicitor, he is a birdwatcher, she is a Baptist, he is black, she is born again, he is gay, she is a mother, he is a criminal, she is an alcoholic, and so on. Life without labels would certainly be difficult, as they are often necessary and sometimes desirable. Yet despite this we must recognize that as soon as we slap a label on a person, our understanding of that individual becomes distorted. We start to see the label rather than the person, and every label, of course, has undertones of approval or disapproval. Furthermore, the connotations these labels hold in our minds are almost always personal to us, carried into the present from our past experiences.

I have to reluctantly admit that for many years I had a very negative view of Irish rugby players. My viewpoint was not based on scientific research or any personal interviews I had conducted. The so-called 'proof' that fuelled my intolerance was that I had once encountered, in a hotel elevator, a solitary member of the Irish national rugby team who refused to talk to me when I engaged him in conversation. Thus my mind concluded that all Irish rugby players were arrogant and unfriendly. My prejudice did not take into account the fact that the poor player's team had just been beaten by my beloved Wales and I was adorned with a Welsh scarf, a Welsh flag, and a blow-up daffodil under my arm! Every day we make judgements on people that will then prejudice our view of those to whom we attach the same label. Whether positive or negative, we are all likely to experience a gut reaction to people's 'labels' – reactions that are forged through our past experiences – and we will all, for example, react very differently to any of the following 'labels' – dad, lawyer, vicar, vegan, therapist, lesbian, Chelsea supporter, Buddhist, divorcee, millionaire. Such a list could, of course, go on and on.

Labels are even used as a convenient way of giving up on somebody – a person is 'lost', 'bad' or 'evil'. On my first visit to our local waste disposal site I was simply amazed at what people were discarding – dozens of TVs, computers, sets of golf clubs, sofas, wardrobes, and so on. We are so quick to give up on things, and it is often cheaper and less hassle to consign things to the rubbish heap than consider repairing them. If something is imperfect, we look to discard and replace. Yet as far as people are concerned, the role of Christians is to model compassion-ate forgiveness, rather than dismiss and discard those who don't reach our moral standards. Our God is the God of second chances, and the New Testament is brimful of stories of people being given that second chance – Simon Peter, Zacchaeus, the prodigal son, Mary Magdalene, St Paul. The suffering servant was, after all, one who came to build and affirm, rather than break and abandon. 'A bruised reed he will not break,' asserts Isaiah 42.3, 'and a smouldering wick he will not snuff out.' We Christians must strive to love and accept people where they are, and then make it possible for them to begin afresh.

In the past I have taken groups of young students to visit a prison for young offenders, as part of a university course on social action. Afterwards the students would reflect on the visit, and every year the different groups of students would report the same experience. Almost all of them would explain that as they chatted to the inmates there was a dawning realization that these young men were not 'evil' or 'bad'. In fact, they were by and large young, energetic people like themselves, with similar interests, dreams and aspirations. The only real difference was that most of the prisoners had either fallen in with the wrong crowd, had been in the wrong place at the wrong time, or had experienced unfortunate childhoods that had influenced their later actions. On one occasion we also took a group to visit a maximum-security prison. Once we had got through various prison checks and been escorted through half a dozen locked gates and doors, we were met by an amicable helper. He sat us all down in a room, served us tea and chatted easily with us. After 20 minutes of friendly conversation, he asked us if we were concerned in any way about our visit. Our students proceeded to tell him how worried they were about actually meeting the inmates face to face, all of whom were incarcerated for serious crimes. 'Well, I'm afraid you're actually talking to one of the bad 'uns right now,' the man said to my stunned students. Before we had realized that he was a 'criminal', we had been able to relate to this man as a fellow human being – we had seen beyond the label to how God saw him: as loved and accepted, whatever his past misdeeds.

We must, then, become aware of the labels that people give themselves, and those that we bestow on others, whether fairly or unfairly. Consequently, as far as possible we must attempt to experience people themselves, rather than experience the labels that we or other people put on them. The Jesuit contemplative Anthony de Mello uses an analogy of a menu in a restaurant. However much we might salivate while perusing the list of food, not one of us will decide to eat the actual menu. The menu is merely an indication of the sumptuous delights that are available. It is the actual food that we want to eat, not the words about the food! Yet most of us proudly affiliate ourselves with certain labels, and some of us would even die for those labels. In reality, however, they are simply words, and therefore mean very little. We are not the actual labels to which we cling jealously, and many of those labels may have the potential to change in an instant. There was a joke that was popular in the 1970s, at the height of the violence in Northern Ireland, about a man walking down a street in Belfast. He suddenly feels a gun pressed to the back of his head. A voice asks, 'Are you a Catholic or a Protestant?' Our protagonist does some quick thinking, and cleverly answers, 'I'm actually a Jew.' And the voice retorts, 'Well, doesn't that just make me the luckiest Arab in the whole of Belfast.'

Freedom comes in letting labels go and accepting that they do not have a hold on us. In reality, Jesus did not reach out to 'gentiles', 'lepers', 'sinners', 'prostitutes' and 'tax collectors'. Those words were merely a convenient way for the Gospel writers to let us know a timeless truth about God's love. Jesus simply reached out to 'people' – a motley collection from all sorts of backgrounds and with a range of life experiences. In the parable of the prodigal son, the father did not immediately label his returning child as 'disrespectful', 'reckless', 'ungrateful', or 'unclean' after working with pigs. Instead, when the father saw his son in the distance, he ran out to greet him, with open arms of love and a heart full of compassion. After all, when compassion is present, labels simply begin to peel away.

Detachment from differences

By appreciating the contribution of both nature and nurture to our lives and by becoming aware of the labels that we ascribe to ourselves and others, we take a step towards detaching ourselves from each other's differences and recognizing our common humanity in God. Dwelling on our differences can, after all, bring not only hatred and conflict but also much anxiety and psychological pain. In her deeply self-aware diary, Etty Hillesum recoils at the memory of the time when seeing a young woman with beautiful legs walk past would remind her of the shortcomings of her own legs, and leave her, she claimed, feeling hopeless and depressed. Many young people today have similar negative feelings about their body image. A recent poll by the *Daily Telegraph* and *Top Sante* found that 90 per cent of women claimed that their bodies made them 'feel down' and they thought about their image every day. In my own experience as a chaplain at a large university, it seems that an increasing number of young men also have similar issues surrounding body dysmorphia, anorexia, bulimia and self-harm. There are certainly no easy answers to help change the present situation, but Hillesum's own release from her oppressive thoughts was the simple act of recognizing her similarities with others, rather than obsessing over the differences.

In the Gospels, Jesus would retreat to isolated places to pray and connect with his Father (for example, Mark 1.35), and by doing so he physically divorced himself from a society where divisions and differences dominated. After all, the 'brood of vipers' that he most fervently opposed in his lifetime were precisely those who saw themselves as 'different' from, and indeed 'better' than, others (Matthew 23.33). Our contemporary world continues to define itself on dissimilarities, whether they are of physical attributes, race, gender, age, nationality, sexuality, religion, class or profession. As a result, discrimination is as rife today as it was 2,000 years ago. We are certainly individuals, and God celebrates our diversity and unique attributes. However, at our core we have many more things in common with our neighbours than those that separate us. Principally, of course, we are united in God's love, which is continually inspiring us to live out our oneness with our neighbours. Thomas Merton famously described a walk he made round the streets in Louisville, Kentucky, during which a great revelation came upon him that all the people he was passing were united in God's love. 'At the corner of Fourth and Walnut, in the centre of the shopping district,' he wrote, 'I was suddenly overwhelmed with the realization that I loved all these people, that they were mine and I theirs, that we could not be alien to one another even though we were total strangers.'

Rather than view the world in this way, however, it is far easier for us to recognize our unity only with those who have similar 'labels' to ours, and to show love merely towards those we recognize as either 'like us' or deserving of our effort. Even Christ himself acknowledged that standing alongside those who are good to us is so much easier than being compassionate towards total strangers or those people we dislike (Matthew 5.43–48). Yet our instinctive reaction to love only those who love us ignores our own faults and our potential for wrongdoing. The BAFTA-nominated film *Of Gods and Men* (2010) tells the true story of a group of Cistercian monks in North Africa who were massacred by terrorists. In the final testament of one of the monks, which was written two years before his violent murder but only opened by his family after his death, he reflected on our common humanity. All of us have the potential for selfless love and compassion, but also a dark and selfish side to our characters. 'I've lived enough to know I am complicit in the evil that, alas, prevails over the world and the evil that will smite me blindly,' wrote Brother Christian. We are, then, no better and no worse than anyone else. This can be a painful realization, as it shatters the world-view that has been drummed into us from childhood. Yet it should rather be wonderfully liberating. We don't differ in who we are from either the most devout saints or the most devious sinners. Rather, we differ in how we decide to act or not to act.

Such a realization can have a very practical effect on our every-day lives. We so easily notice the unpleasant side of our work colleagues, our friends or our family members. Rather than this leading us towards intolerance and judgementalism, however, it should help us to recognize our own weaknesses, many of which may not be clear to us but are probably blatantly obvious to people close to us! Thus we become inspired to feel not guilt about our own imperfections but compassion about the imperfections that we identify in others. It is by taking such a step that we begin to view others not through our own eyes but through Christ's eyes. We can be led to extend our compassion to *everyone* – even to strangers we meet, those we actively dislike, and those who are hateful or aggressive towards us. By enlarging our circle of compassion we reach out from our small, inward-looking world towards embracing the whole of humankind.

Our role as Christians, then, is to live out the role of the compassionate father of the prodigal son. We often relate to the errant son in that parable, and we sometimes fear that we might be the jealous older brother. But God is calling us to join him as the running father, who loves and welcomes even his most rebellious, abandoned or lost children. As physician Paul Tournier wrote, considering a friend who was going through a divorce:

> The circumstances of our lives are different, but the reality of our hearts is the same. If I were in his place, would I act any differently from him? I have no idea. At least I know that I should need friends who loved me unreservedly just as I am, with all my weaknesses, and who would trust me without judging me.

Sadly, it is often the case that neither our churches nor our lives exhibit such a grace-full and compassionate attitude. Most of us can find a reason, biblical or otherwise, why a certain person or particular group of people can be viewed as unwelcome or undesirable. Yet we should be modelling a kingdom where no prodigal son is unwelcome and there are no undesirables. Christ's community should be a community of colourful and wonderful so-called 'labels', all made in the image of the Father – black, white, rich, poor, homeless, mentally ill, single parent, gay people, physically disabled, divorced, depressed, transgendered, drug-addicted, unemployed. Jesus did not turn his back on people; he welcomed them with open arms in the shape of a cross.

7

Reverence for life

————◆•◆•◆————

Animals were no more put on this earth for the use of
human beings, than women were put here for men, or black
people were put here for white people.

Alice Walker

Each creature is but a patterned gradation of one great
harmonious whole.

J. W. von Goethe

In the Dreamworks film *How to Train your Dragon* (2010),
the lead character, Hiccup, has from an early age been taught
that his own people, the Vikings, kill dragons. Their instinct to
destroy these magnificent flying creatures is, explains his teacher,
simply part of their nature and as such it cannot be changed.
Later in the film, however, Hiccup finds an injured dragon and
discovers deep feelings of care and compassion towards him,
and rebels against the long-standing Viking tradition by refusing to kill the helpless beast. 'I wouldn't kill him because he
looked as frightened as I was,' he explains to his girlfriend
Astrid. 'I looked at him and I saw myself.' When we recognize
the incarnational presence of Christ in the world around us,
we are certainly challenged to see ourselves in other people,
animals, and even trees and plants. Thus Christ's command to
'Do to others as you would have them do to you' is expanded
to everything that has been gifted with life.

My dad grew up on a small farm on Anglesey in North Wales.
He recounts that he would often be required to drown unwanted
animals. On one occasion my Taid (grandfather) sent him to

destroy a number of newborn kittens. Ten minutes later my Taid found my father by the water cistern, the kittens having been successfully disposed of, but my father had now moved on to trying to drown his screaming two-year-old brother! My father maintains that his first and only venture into 'attempted murder' reflected the fact that his frequent job of ending the lives of animals had warped the value he put on life in general. The author Leonard Woolf, husband of Virginia Woolf, recalls how as a child he was also given the task of drowning a number of small unwanted animals. As he held a puppy under the water, the newborn creature fought for its life. Woolf later wrote that during the act he underwent a slow realization that each animal was an individual, an 'I', that was fighting for survival as desperately as any of us would. 'It was a horrible, an uncivilized thing to drown that "I" in a bucket of water,' he recalled.

Yet we live in a world in which we rarely recognize that non-human forms of life are worthy of the compassion and respect we bestow on fellow humans. Instead, our own selfish over-consumption ignores the detrimental effect that we are having on our environment and the plethora of life forms around us. It is no excuse to say, 'that's the way it's always been'. There has never been a valid justification for slavery, misogyny, racism or homophobia, and there is, likewise, no valid justification for the way we have in the past treated both our environment and non-human forms of life. As Sue Gerhardt writes in her best-seller *The Selfish Society*, 'Like children let loose in the sweet shop, we have gorged ourselves on everything we could get hold of, blissfully unaware of the true cost of our activities.'

Is life really about 'me'?

Thomas Hobbes speculated in his *Leviathan* that human life is generally antagonistic, being a 'war of all against all'. While Christians must affirm that the true state of humankind is harmony with God and each other, the traditional doctrine of original sin also teaches us that we are presently, in some fundamental way, disconnected from God, from our fellow human beings and from the natural world around us. Each of us is an individual bundle of fears, desires and passions that demand to be satisfied or quelled. The world around us often serves to affirm this belief that life is about us as individuals. In fact, Cartesian thought, centred on the principle of 'I think therefore I am', leads us to conclude that life is about one specific individual alone – 'me'. Each day we become wholly absorbed in our own little world, truly believing that 'I' am the only important thing in creation.

According to St Augustine, this attitude of self-centred individuality is what is at the root of 'sin'. He describes it as a state of mind where we are 'caved in on ourselves' (*incurvatus in se*). Our souls, which should lead us to harmony with the people around us, with the natural world and with God himself, are turned inwards, as we focus on ourselves alone. Christ offers us a chance to be liberated from this self-centred and selfish condition, however, and it is an amazingly freeing realization to grasp the reality that life is not actually about 'me'. In his song 'Chicago', the folk-rock singer-songwriter Sufjan Stevens expresses this desire 'for freedom from myself'. Yet such a freedom comes at a great cost, as we have to abandon deeply held convictions that are rooted in our very earliest years. I remember finding my daughter, who had just started school, crying in the corner of the room, after she'd fallen out with her cousin of the same age. 'I didn't realize that I wasn't the boss of everyone,' she whispered as I comforted her.

The belief that we are actually more important than others around us certainly begins in our childhood, but it continues into our adulthood. We very often act as if life is simply about ourselves. In general elections, for example, we all ask the question of how the policies of the parties might affect us personally – taxes, health, education, immigration, and so on. How many of us would vote for a party whose principal emphasis had no impact on us whatsoever? Or would we vote for a party that would seemingly have a negative impact on our situation? All this despite the fact that recent studies, chronicled by Richard Wilkinson and Kate Pickett in *The Spirit Level*, have shown that whether we are rich or poor, we would be more happy and content if we lived in a fairer, more equal society.

The strong emotions we have that persuade us that life is all about 'me' have a biological foundation. We have inherited neurological systems that stimulate a strong sense of self-preservation. Without this, we would never have survived as a species. However, our brains also include the neocortex, which gives us the power of reasoning and thus helps us to question and even discard our more primitive instincts. When we let go of our deeply held belief that we are the most important thing in the world, we can begin to recognize the value and significance of all creation and start to truly feel for the suffering of our fellow human beings as well as that of creatures and of the environment around us. Many religions touch upon this concept when they refer to 'putting the self to death'. This does not imply any self-loathing or guilt, nor should it entail becoming obsessed with our failings. Rather, it is the movement towards dethroning ourselves from the centre of our world, and putting 'the other' in our place.

In order to change our ways and thought-patterns, instilled in us from an early age, we need, in the words of Ignatius of Loyola, to 'act in the contrary direction of our sin' (*agere contra*). In other words, we need to move away from our 'me-first' mentality and start thinking about the larger world outside, rather than be fixated with our own smaller worlds inside. Consequently, we are drawn to the realization that everything in our wonderful world has value and import – from the strangers we pass on the street, to our pets who share our houses, to the squirrels who dart across our paths in the park, to the snowdrops breaking through the soil in our gardens, and even the slugs under the stones. Everything is created by God and is therefore inherently valuable and has a right to life. 'Can it be true that a monkey's playfulness and the song of a cricket make God happy?' asks Swedish contemplative Annika Spalde.

Reverence for life

When we begin to find such a solidarity and affinity with the natural world, we are certainly treading on holy ground and we connect with the foundation of all being. As such, our only response can be esteem and compassion for life in all its manifest forms. After all, if creation is a unified whole, then each of its individual parts is deserving of our love and attention. The German phrase that philosopher and medical missionary Albert Schweitzer used to express this concept is '*Ehrfurcht vor dem Leben*', which is often translated as 'reverence for life'. The word *Ehrfurcht*, however, expresses far more than its English translation implies. It suggests an attitude of awe and ultimate respect, and thus carries with it an overwhelming sense of moral responsibility towards life and all of creation.

For Schweitzer this was no abstract intellectualism. His principle of 'reverence for life' came to him through practical experience, as he worked among the sick in the heart of tropical Africa. While Richard Dawkins maintains that cruelty in nature is one of the main stumbling blocks of belief in the divine, it was not a sanitized version of nature that led Schweitzer to his God-centred conclusion. Rather, when he was surrounded by suffering and death, both in the hospital in which he worked and in the unforgiving and cruel natural world of the jungle around him, he came to regard a transcendent 'reverence for life' as the only way of living that made sense. Nature may well be 'red in tooth and claw', to use Alfred Lord Tennyson's phrase, but we have been gifted with the potential to bring compassion and love to the pain and suffering we witness.

At the heart of the concept of reverence for life is interconnectedness. All of life is related in some amazing way, and thus we should be able to empathize with all suffering, whether human or not. 'The tiny beetle that lies dead in your path – it was a living creature,' wrote Schweitzer, 'struggling for existence like yourself, rejoicing in the sun like you, knowing fear and pain like you.' Most of us already regard human life as inherently important, but rarely do we value the lives of non-human creatures. Every creature will itself hold to the importance of its own life, albeit unconsciously, and this realization should lead us to solidarity with all forms of life – forms of life that are just like us. In this sense, our relationship with nature is far more intimate than we might think: 'Wherever you see life,' wrote Schweitzer, 'that is yourself!' Our profound bond with other living creatures should inspire us to remove the false dichotomy between us and the natural world. This is Jesus' core teaching on love applied to an interconnected world – 'the ethic of love widened into universality', as Schweitzer himself put it. Love's principal focus should be the promotion of life and thus we should aim, as best we can, to preserve it.

The inwardness of things

The concept of reverence for life helps us, as Christians, to recognize the infinite value of all created living things, yet the materialistic world in which we live patently regards 'life' very differently. According to E. F. Schumacher, in his philo-sophical treatise *A Guide for the Perplexed*, science, economics and politics deal only with the surface value of the world around us. A cow is not seen as inherently valuable in itself, but rather as 'meat' to be sold and consumed. Likewise, the factory worker is not valued as a human being, but is viewed as a unit of labour. Too often the pursuit of economic growth, efficiency and productivity is regarded as more valuable than our fellow human beings or the natural world. Schumacher suggests that, in fact, every living thing has a transcendent meaning that cannot be grasped by the heartless logic of science or the manipulative nature of politics. In other words, it is 'the inwardness of things', the mysterious quality of every living being, that gives them their value. 'Anything that we can destroy but are unable to make,' writes Schumacher, 'is, in a sense, sacred, and all our "explanations" of it do not explain anything.'

Our first step, then, is to go beyond seeing each other in purely physical terms. We are not simply beings to be viewed in the context of our usefulness. In *Small is Beautiful*, an earlier work by Schumacher, he championed the importance of the metaphysical – from the Greek *meta*, to go behind, and *physika*, physical matter; and that is exactly what he is calling us to do: to look beyond the physical. Yet materialism and the prevailing mechanistic world-view of Cartesianism have marginalized metaphysics, and so 'meaning' beyond something's practical use is hard for us to accept. 'We have seemed to ask – is it profitable?' said Archbishop Desmond Tutu at the World Economic Forum in Switzerland in 2009. 'God is saying what we ought to have been asking – is it right?'

When we can recognize that we ourselves have a meaning beyond our physical qualities, we will be drawn to relate that meaning to the 'other' in the broadest sense of the word. Our anthropocentricism has warped our view of the natural world. The reality is that even at a basic level we do not perceive the intrinsic natures of individual objects when we look at them, but rather we view each thing from our own peculiarly human perspective. When we look at a flower, for example, we may think that it is beautiful and colourful, and may appreciate its pleasant aroma. Other creatures, though, will perceive a flower according to their own particular make-up – for insects it is pollen and nectar; bats 'see' a flower as ultrasound, snakes as infrared. Once we accept our anthropological way of viewing the world, we may find it easier to identify the true worth of each and every aspect of creation.

The present *status quo*, however, means that to most of us even higher organisms are regarded as having no real value in themselves, save their worth to us humans. Animals are regarded as having no tangible interests or rights. Richard Holloway suggests that many animals in modern industrial farming experience a 'double-dying', as their everyday existence is as pitiful as the death they are destined to undergo. They live out their wretched lifespans in 'crowded disease-prone torture', at the end of which they may be transported hundreds of miles in overcrowded trucks to their slaughter. Even their carcases are rarely treated with respect. A friend of mine worked in an abattoir during his school's summer breaks, and recalls the utter contempt of the staff towards the animals there, with bizarre and tasteless games being played with the body parts of animals, especially the genitalia. But our society continues to turn a blind eye towards heartless factory farming practices. Often they are not only tolerated but justified with the argument that animals are little more than unfeeling machines who don't really 'suffer' in the human sense of the word. 'Who hears when animals cry?' asked The Smiths on their 1985 single 'Meat is Murder', and in the song they compare the whines of heifers to human cries of pain and suffering. Yet in reality, to most of us today these whines are, in the words of Descartes, 'no more than the creaking of a wheel'.

I–Thou relationships

According to Martin Buber there are two kinds of relationship. He defines the first as an 'I–It relationship', where the association between two bodies is impersonal, unfeeling and distant, as it is primarily concerned with what the 'I' can get out of the 'It'. This is a relationship largely of expediency, which often descends into manipulation or control. In our everyday lives we regularly engage in I–It relationships – with shop assistants, workers in banks, and waiters in cafes and restaurants. We may well not consciously view these individuals as people, but rather as a means of getting what we want. As consumers, our interest in their well-being is minimal, whereas their efficiency and competence are important to us.

Buber's second type of relationship in our lives is the 'I–Thou relationship' – associations that are personal, respectful and engaging, and have at their heart a sense of care and compassion for the other. Most I–Thou relationships are with family members and friends, although there is no reason why we can't expand this I–Thou sphere to include people beyond our immediate circle, as well as other living creatures and the natural world. After all, compassion is not just about the human experience, but is rooted in our togetherness with the whole created order. The kingdom of God is centred on the recreation of all life, and not merely concerned with human individuals or society at large.

An I–Thou attitude to the world is commonly found in the arts. Michael Morpurgo's books, for example, have inspired thousands of young people, and with the successful adaptation of his novel *War Horse* to the big screen by Steven Spielberg, will surely continue to do so. Throughout his numerous novels runs a deeply spiritual sense of respect and regard for the other, whether that 'other' is human or animal. As one character in *War Horse* puts it, when gazing at the magnificent animal:

> I tell you, my friend, there's divinity in a horse, and specially in a horse like this. God got it right the day he created them. And to find a horse like this in the middle of this filthy abomination of a war, is for me like finding a butterfly on a dung heap.

For Morpurgo, this emphasis on I–Thou-ness is more than mere words on paper, as his whole life reflects an attitude to the wonder of life in all its manifest forms. In 1974, before his books began to be published, he and his wife set up the charity Farms for City Children, which aimed to give deprived children from inner-city areas the chance to experience the countryside. Through staying at a working farm, they would learn, in the words of the charity itself, 'where their food comes from, the importance of caring for animals and the land, and the value of working co-operatively as a team'. Thus the children are rewarded in a non-material and life-giving manner. The charity today runs three farms in the UK, and Morpurgo is still renowned for his wide-ranging charitable work for the care of children and animals, including being ambassador for Save the Children. It is clear that there is a spirituality that drives his care and concern for those who have no voice of their own. His biography notes that from a very young age he was drawn to the figure of Jesus and he would spend many hours in his school's chapel. 'I wanted to believe,' he revealingly comments, 'I still do.' It is of little surprise that Ted Hughes, his close friend and then poet laureate, wrote in a poem that 'God rides in the wind' above the farm for city children at Treginnis Isaf, near St David's in Pembrokeshire, Wales.

The I–Thou experience, then, is present when we connect with the transcendent in our lives, whether that is through human beings or our relationships with animals, plants and our environment. We need to make the decision, however, to view everything we come into contact with in an I–Thou way and treat them accordingly. Our attitude towards the world around us is highly subjective and personal, and we ourselves decide, often subconsciously, whether to manipulate and control things or to value and care for them. 'You are wrong if you think that the joy of life comes principally from human relationships,' muses Emile Hirsch in *Into the Wild* (2007), as he contemplates a breathtaking panoramic view. 'God has placed it all around us, it's in everything and it's in anything we can experience – people just need to change the way they look at things.'

In this sense, we can even forge I–Thou relationships with manmade materials. In some of his poetry R. S. Thomas portrays how in the twentieth century the deep relationship farmers had with nature was transferred to the new, shining machines that they began to use. 'Gone the old look that yoked him to the soil, He's a new man now, part of the machine, His nerves of metal and his blood oil', Thomas asserts in 'Cynddylan on a Tractor'. There is a similar theme in the French film *The Eighth Day* (1996), where the final scene details an alternative six days of creation, with the principal character Jean coming to experience a deep appreciation and awareness of numerous aspects of life. The film earlier shows how a young Down's syndrome man leads Jean away from I–It associations towards I–Thou relationships in his life. Then, in the six days of creation, God is said to have created various aspects of the natural world – the sun, wind, water, clouds, trees, grass, cows, and men, women and children – but also manmade inventions, which have their own beauty and power. 'The fifth day he made planes,' Jean asserts. 'If you don't take them, you can watch them fly past.' Experiences of I–Thou-ness, then, are rooted in our own perception of the world, but when we recognize the interconnectedness of the universe it is in the wonder and beauty of life in all its manifest forms that gives the I–Thou relationship its full significance.

Faith and the wonder of life

The prevailing materialist world-view of our society attempts to persuade us that things around us can be 'possessed' – they are to be competed for, purchased, or owned. Once we recognize the essential unity of all living beings, however, we will see that life can never be considered a commodity. Even our pets are not owned by us, despite the fact that we may have paid for them originally. All living things exist in their own right, and from the moment we are born we are intricately bound up and belong to one another in the mystery of being. God showed to Julian of Norwich a small thing, the size of a hazelnut, in the palm of a hand, and told her that this was the whole of creation. Our beautiful interrelatedness has the divine at its heart. In the words of Julian of Norwich, our universe 'lasts and always shall, because God loves it; and so everything has being by the love of God'.

Yet in both the natural world and the sphere of human relations, we are facing times of great disorder and devastation. In
the 1995 papal encyclical *Evangelium Vitae* Pope John Paul II
referred to the 'culture of death' of the modern world. We are
not only shockingly merciless towards each other, but we extend
our cruelty to the creatures with which we share the planet.
Rarely are even farmed animals treated with the respect and
dignity that farmers of old used to give their livestock. In the
large global corporations that dominate the food industry, cows,
hens and sheep are viewed as products to be reared to supply
fast-food outlets. They are bred specifically for death. Richard
Holloway points out that while nature itself is cruel, God has
at least endowed every living creature with a fighting instinct
for survival, and a means to achieve it that may include armour,
speed, disguise, poison or odour. We humans, however, offer
no chance for these defensive capabilities to be used. Nothing
is as uncaring and ruthless in nature as the hungry human.

Whether or not this recognition should lead us to vegetarianism is to be debated. Albert Schweitzer was a proponent
of vegetarianism, although he ate meat on occasions. Perhaps
the indigenous hunting communities of our world today can
help us to bridge the gap between reverence for life and the
killing of animals for food. While they are principally carnivores
in their food habits, many of these communities hold a great
affinity for the prey they hunt and appreciate their utter
dependence on the animals that are sacrificed so that their
people might live and thrive. There is a definite empathy and
affection towards the hunted. In fact, compassionate ceremonies
and rituals are often performed to show gratitude to the animals
for the gift of their lives. The tribesmen of the Kalahari Desert
in southern Africa will, for example, symbolically enter into
the suffering of their dying prey by enacting their final death
throes. Contrast this with our own food system, which is largely
controlled by a small group of multinational corporations who
attempt to hide the truth about what we are eating and the

harsh treatment of both animals and workers in their factories. 'In the meat aisle, there are no bones any more,' comments the Oscar-nominated film *Food, Inc.* (2008). 'There is this deliberate veil, this curtain, drawn between us and where our food is coming from.'

Other indigenous communities carry out rituals showing their gratitude in the collection and receiving of produce from animals. The honey-hunters in the state of Kedah in Malaysia enact a ritual in which they pray, sing songs and bathe before they go in search of the Giant Bee hives in the tall Tualang trees of the region's rainforest. Their attitude of care and gratitude towards both the bees and the dense forest is vastly different from that of some large-scale, non-organic beekeepers in the West, who view honey simply as a commodity and employ exploitative methods such as unnatural feed, chemical treatments and artificial insemination of the queen bee, so that they can aim at producing as much profit as possible.

A reverence for food is a natural consequence of the recognition that other life forms have as much right to breathe the air of our globe as we do. Science is, in fact, increasingly showing us that other creatures are not so different from us, and our DNA does not differ vastly from other species. The 2011 documentary film *Project Nim* charted an experiment in the USA in the mid 1970s where a chimpanzee was breastfed by a female caretaker and taught sign language. The aim was to find out whether an animal could communicate with us if it were raised like a human being. By the age of five Nim had a vocabulary of more than 120 words. 'He grew on you quick,' noted one of his carers, 'he was so charming. It didn't occur to me that animals had that kind of personality like ours.' The Oscar-winning director James Marsh explained in an interview how his own attitude towards non-human life developed during the filming. 'My view of animals has changed,' he explained. 'My understanding of them has changed very much, particularly as regards their intelligence and, dare I say it, their sensibilities.

Higher primates clearly feel things in the same way that we feel things.'

Yet as Christians we should go one step further, and recognize that all parts of creation, whether or not they are physiologic- ally close to us, are equally worthy of our attention, respect and love. All life wills to live, just as we ourselves do. We must appreciate that this will and drive are gifted by the creator and should, therefore, be taken seriously. Embracing this view will have huge implications on moral and ethical matters – not least on our attitudes towards the environment, food production, health care, emerging technologies, animal care, energy devel- opment, and so on. 'Do not do any injury, if you can possibly avoid it,' the great Welsh Celtic saint Teilo is purported to have said while reflecting on creation. 'Sin', then, is when we seek to destroy that which God wishes to live, while doing 'good' is when we actively promote and preserve life. Thus the old anthropocentric, human-centred paradigm does not reflect a truly Christian world-view. If creation is a unified whole, then the individual parts deserve our attention and compassion, not because they are useful or beneficial to us, but simply for their own sake. The whole web of life is valued and loved by God, not merely one strand of it.

This recognition leads us towards the question of whether there is an order of priority among life forms. Who wins, for example, when we are forced, for whatever reason, to decide between the fate of two animals from different species? Or who is the victor when it is a choice between human survival and the survival of an animal? To put it in very crude terms, if I saw a lion about to maul you to death, should I shoot it? Or should I happily allow the giant creature to feast on its tasty meal? Even Christ himself, of course, recognized that we humans will naturally have some kind of scale of priority; he asserted that we are 'worth more than many sparrows' (Luke 12.7). Yet in the very same passage Jesus gives credence to the universal principle of reverence for life, as he affirms how important nature is in God's eyes – sparrows, ravens and lilies. It is, after all, God's love for living things that gives them their ultimate worth. Schweitzer always refused to speculate about an 'order of priority' for God's creatures. For him the whole concept for 'reverence for life' would be devalued by the formation of a strict set of rules. However, he realized that there would be times in our lives when practical decisions regarding the relative values of living creatures would have to be made, not least because the food chain necessitates that some have to die that others may live. He concluded that while such decisions of priority should be personal to each individual, they should always be grounded in reverence and compassion.

Moving away from our past

The concept of a profound reverence towards living things is to be found in many of the world faiths, from the emphasis on non-violence (*ahimsa*) in Hinduism, Jainism and Buddhism, to the Muslim mystic Bawa Muhaiyaddeen who was reminded by a talking deer that people and animals were created from the same material and so should be treated with respect. Yet the fact that such a concept is at the heart of our own Christian faith is often ignored by the faithful. *The Green Bible*, published in 2008 and with introductory articles by such high-profile scholars as N. T. Wright, Desmond Tutu and Pope John Paul II, is a version of the Bible with passages about creation care highlighted in green ink. Even a brief perusal of these sections, of which there are more than 1,000, shows that Scripture unequivocally advocates loving ethical guidelines for all of creation. Old Testament laws, for example, prohibit the sport of hunting, and the slaughter of animals for food is permitted only within strict guidelines that ensure the least suffering for the animals. Even the Sabbath should include rest for domestic animals as well as humans (Exodus 20.10). 'In an act without parallel in civilization,' writes Jewish scholar Leo Baeck, 'the

Bible placed animals under the protection of laws devised for man.' Furthermore, the wisdom tradition describes divine Wisdom as being embedded in creation (Job 12.7–10). It seems clear from Scripture that God loves animals for their own sake – a fact that biblical scholars inform us was quite possibly unique among the deities of the ancient Near East.

This revolutionary attitude continued among some Christian thinkers and theologians through the centuries. 'Every single creature is full of God,' wrote Meister Eckhart, 'and is a book about God.' Peruvian saint Martin de Porres took the concept of a universal brotherhood a step further than Charles de Foucauld was to do three centuries later. De Porres regarded *all* living creatures, including animals, as God's children, and so urged us to be protectors of our brothers and sisters. After all, when we are violent towards somebody or something we affirm our differences, whether that is in race, religion, politics or even species. With the concept of reverence for life, we reject separation in favour of harmony and unity, by offering our full compassion and love to the other.

Still, in many Christian circles today there is not even a basic recognition of the preciousness of all created species, so shackled are we by our dualistic world-view and by a misreading of the stewardship command in the creation narratives. There is a general Christian attitude that views animals as qualitatively different from us humans. In fact, they are often perceived as being little more than animated machines for our own use and appropriation, and we regard them, albeit often unconsciously, as having no real rights alongside us here on the planet. I faced this kind of attitude among work colleagues when they discovered I had sponsored an orang-utan through the World Wide Fund for Nature (WWF). Several people expressed their disapproval, asserting that my money would be better spent on 'humans who are suffering, rather than insentient animals'. Such a viewpoint is founded on the mistaken philosophy that humankind is the only important living creature; it also fails to acknowledge the basic interconnectedness of our biosphere. Essentially, I was not sponsoring an actual orang-utan (everyone who sponsors an orang-utan receives exactly the same letter, detailing the same orang-utan called 'Keira'). The sponsorship money goes towards ensuring that the rainforests of Borneo are saved from the threat of destruction as humans harvest the trees for palm oil. By protecting the rainforests we are not only saving the natural habitat of the orang-utan, we are also ensuring that future generations of our own species are left a greener and healthier environment.

Our planet's destiny, then, is related directly to our treatment of our fellow species. God can entice us and draw us towards coexisting harmoniously, but ultimately we have free will and therefore are able to go against God's desire for his beloved creation. Christians have in the past not always been good stewards of creation, using their power to control, manipulate and exploit the natural world. This is the opposite of what Christ himself taught about the relinquishing of power. Our role is to prioritize compassion towards 'the other', and in doing so to model a different kind of power in our dealings with nature. Thus we aim to support and sustain life rather than dominate and destroy it. This is true reverence for the wonderful miracle of life in all its countless forms. 'Since we cannot give life,' stated eighteenth-century Quaker Joshua Evans, 'let us be careful not to take it.' We are, after all, the one species who can make a difference to the world around us. Schweitzer pictured all animals living in the darkness of ignorance, with humankind as the only creature able to glimpse the reality at the centre of the universe – that all life is precious. From our anthropomorphic viewpoint, the concept of the 'sanctity of life', when used in ethical debates, is reserved for humans alone. In God's eyes, however, all life is sacred.

Epilogue: everyday compassion

I know we are all pretty small in the big scheme of things, and I suppose the most you can hope for is to make some kind of difference. But what kind of difference have I made? What in the world is better because of me?

> *Jack Nicholson in* About Schmidt *(2002)*

Who seeks for heaven alone to save his soul,
May keep the path, but will not reach the goal;
While he who walks in love may wander far,
Yet God will bring him where the blessed are.

> *Henry Van Dyke*, The Other Wise Man

Matthew's Gospel describes the wise men visiting the manger of Christ, to give their gifts of gold, frankincense and myrrh. In 1896 a short novel by Henry Van Dyke, *The Other Wise Man*, told the tale of a fourth Magi, who had a pearl as a gift for the Christ-child. Artaban misses the birth of Christ because he stops on the way to help a dying man. He then spends 33 years trying to find the Messiah, but is continually hindered by the fact that he stops to help people who are suffering. When Artaban finally arrives in Jerusalem he is told that Christ is about to be crucified. He begins to make his way hastily to Golgotha, outside the walls of the city, to offer his pearl as a ransom to set Jesus free. As he rushes through the Damascus gate out of the city, however, he sees a young girl being persecuted by a group of soldiers, and he pauses 'to look at her with compassion'. It is here that he feels 'the old conflict of his soul . . . the conflict between the expectation of faith and the impulse of love'. His compassion leads him to offer his pearl to save the helpless girl. At that point the great earthquake that occurred at Jesus' death causes a tile to fall from a roof and strike Artaban on the head. As he lies dying in the arms of the young girl he had freed, he imagines the spirit of Christ and mutters, 'Three-and-thirty years have I looked for thee; but I have never seen thy face, nor ministered to thee, my King.' He and the girl then hear a sweet voice, although there is no one close to them: 'Verily I say unto thee, inasmuch as thou hast done it unto one of the least of these my brethren, thou hast done it unto me.' Van Dyke, then, is saying that compassion is far more important than any outward religious observance or strict doctrinal confession. Compassion is, as the gift that Artaban seeks to give intimates, the 'pearl of great price' of Jesus' parable (Matthew 13.45–46).

The words spoken as Artaban dies are, of course, from a key incarnational passage. Matthew 25.31–46 reveals much about the importance of our actions. Yet churches down the years have often diluted that message. The passage describes God separating the sheep from the goats as a result of either their action or their inaction, and it stands as the only time that Jesus talks specifically about a dual outcome in the afterlife. Practical compassion is, then, at the crux of the gospel. When we are present to those who suffer, standing alongside them in their suffering, God is also present. Sometimes, though, the Reformation's emphasis on justification by faith alone seems to make us hesitant to affirm that our actions are also vitally important. Martin Luther even wanted to remove the epistle of James from the canon of the New Testament – the 'epistle of straw' as he called it – so central is the importance of action to its thesis. Yet we need to be wary of rooting our faith simply on a strict criterion of 'belief'. Faith is not a 'tick list', where we are judged to be either sound or heretical, and God is not someone we merely 'believe in'. Rather, faith is opening our eyes to the incarnation flowing from the world around us and God is a relationship that changes our lives. The question of what we believe should never outweigh the question of whether we compassionately live out God in our daily lives.

This does not, of course, invalidate the concept of justification by faith, but simply completes it. Our actions do not bring us closer to God's love, as God's love cannot be brought any closer to us than it is already. It is only our acceptance and recognition of that love that is in question. As such, our emphasis on compassionate action must include compassion towards ourselves for when we fail to live lives of love. We must ask forgiveness for our shortcomings, but make sure that we truly let go of our failures and wrongdoings. Much of my pastoral work, especially with university students, centres on dealing with the guilt and self-hatred that people experience in relation to actions both taken and not taken. The Christian faith is a liberating faith, which urges us to accept forgiveness from the divine and then move forward. Our calling as Christians is not to be shackled by the chains of our past, but to allow the liberating and unconditional love of God to inspire us to follow in the footsteps of Jesus in everything we say and do.

Merely talking about the gospel will never be enough. 'Poor little talkative Christianity,' E. M. Forster perceptively observed in *A Passage to India*. Living out the gospel is what faith is really about. As Albert Schweitzer put it, on reflecting on his Christian ministry as a medic:

> I wanted to be a doctor that I might be able to work without having to talk. For years I have been giving myself out in words . . . This new form of activity I could not represent to myself as being talking about the religion of love, but only as an actual putting it into practice.

I came to a similar realization after many years spent teaching doctrinal theology at college and university. I eventually returned to learning to study practical theology at Oxford. At that time I was able to bring my previously theoretical understanding of theology to bear on every part of my life and especially on the work I was doing with people such as fearful and tearful asylum-seekers about to be deported back home, university students mourning the suicide of a 19-year-old friend, the increasing numbers of homeless on the streets of Washington

DC where I was based one summer, and the dying and bereaved in local hospitals and hospices. I soon came to the conclusion that all my waxing lyrical about theology in the previous 15 years was fruitless without practical action. Compassion, after all, is not about words. It is a way of being that is centred on doing. The challenge in our often cynical world is not to concentrate on persuading people about 'the truth' of our dogmas, but to live out that very truth in our everyday lives.

We should not be fooled into believing that compassion is simply about results. 'Success is not a name of God,' wrote Martin Buber. We live in a consumer-driven society that is obsessed with competition, success and achievements. We so often judge our actions on whether they are successful or not, and if there is little chance of success we do not see any point in our undertakings. Compassion, however, is not in the business of quantifiable results, statistics or qualitative evidence. While the *Christus Victor* theory of the atonement presents the crucifixion as a time of joyful victory, it was, in worldly terms at least, a terrible and dark defeat. Yet without the agony of the cross there would be no glory at the resurrection. Both our realization of the interconnectedness of the world and our confidence that God is love in his very essence are a guarantee that no act of compassion, however small, is pointless. Thomas Merton, who vigorously opposed the Vietnam War in the mid 1960s, wrote that in God's eyes any action taken in the spirit of compassion does not depend on success. 'As you get used to this idea,' he concluded, 'you start more and more to concentrate not on the results but on the value, the rightness, the truths of the work itself.' Success, then, is of no significance to a compassionate heart, as we assert with Meister Eckhart that we simply 'act so that we may act'.

In the Oscar-winning documentary *Man on Wire* (2008), the French tightrope walker Philippe Petit reflects on his death-defying but illegal high-wire routine between the twin towers of the World Trade Center in 1974. Following his arrest for his breathtaking 45-minute stunt, the media clamoured to interview him, desperate to know why he had embarked on such a treacherous feat. 'Why? Why? That was a very American thing, that question,' he later reflected. 'I did something magnificent and mysterious and I got a particular "why?", and the beauty of it is that I didn't have any "why"!' Compassion is similarly something magnificent and mysterious, and it does not require any reason or justification except that it draws us closer to the very reason of our existence. By showing compassion towards the world around us we may well discover that the very meaning and fulfilment we have been seeking in our own lives follows. Research has shown that those people who spend time standing alongside and caring for others are mentally and physically healthier, and do better socially and economically, than those who lack interpersonal moral sensibilities. When we give, we get so much back ourselves!

Still, we will sometimes face moments when our compassion seems pointless or disheartening. It is then that we should hold on to the fact that the greatest tragedy in life is not failure. The greatest tragedy, as Joseph Campbell pointed out, is for us to climb the ladder of success only to discover that we've been climbing up the wrong wall. When we practise compassion, we are always climbing the correct wall, and while that climb may sometimes be arduous and seemingly impossible, as Christians we always affirm the miracle of resurrection – that light can break through darkness and life can conquer death. 'There is no situation that is not transfigurable,' asserted Desmond Tutu, 'there is no situation of which we can say this is absolutely, totally void of hope.' We are, after all, part of a greater whole, and when we stand in compassionate solidarity with each other and with the rest of creation we will always witness new life and resurrection. God's spirit continues to work for the good, even if we cannot always see the results of our efforts. We trust, then, that our compassionate acts will have effects that transcend their outward success or failure. Thus we can stand with Brett Anderson, the lead singer of the rock group Suede; when he was asked what the point of life was, he answered, 'to have written a plus sign, no matter how big or small'.

Our opportunities for compassionate acts should therefore be seen as part and parcel of God's providence. God wills us into compassionate actions. 'God is not only behind us in pursuit,' writes Robert Barron, 'but also ahead of us in allurement, like a mother urging her child to take his first step.' Every event that happens, and every encounter we have, should not be regarded as pure coincidence, but rather as an opportunity for us to align ourselves to divine compassion and help bring about new life and resurrection. We need, then, to cultivate an awareness and an attentiveness to the world around us, by opening our eyes, ears and hearts to opportunities where we can bring compassion to events and situations – to feed the hungry, visit the sick or imprisoned, sit and talk with the lonely, speak for those with no voice, defend the defenceless and care for our surroundings.

The first words on Nick Cave's critically acclaimed album *The Boatman's Call* assert that he does not believe in 'an interventionist God'. Cave later sang the same song, 'Into My Arms', at the funeral of INXS lead singer Michael Hutchence. St Paul, however, in his letter to the Philippians, suggests a middle way between a God who 'interferes' in our everyday lives and a God who is distant and impersonal. 'It is God who works in you to will and to act in order to fulfil his good purpose' (Philippians 2.13). God, then, is 'an intentionalist God', who continually makes his compassionate intention discernible to us. The challenge of our quest is, therefore, to recognize his loving intention and then to live our lives in tune with it. Christ is certainly not impotent in our suffering world, but he looks for us to complete his will and thus to ensure that compassion and love set our beautifully interconnected world alight. Petit, when pushed further on the reason why he had risked his life on the high-wire walk at the World Trade Center in the early hours of 7 August 1974, said: 'When I see three oranges, I juggle; when I see two towers, I walk.' Likewise, our awareness of Christ in the people we meet and in the world around us should lead us to assert: 'When I see suffering, I reach out in compassion.'

Bibliography

Many of the quotations I have used in this book have been collected over many years from films, books, newspapers, music lyrics, reliable internet sources and television programmes. However, to give readers the opportunity to explore topics further, I include here a bibliography of the principal texts that were used in the writing of the book.

Karen Armstrong, *In the Beginning: A New Reading of Genesis* (Fount, London 1998)

Karen Armstrong, *Twelve Steps to a Compassionate Life* (Bodley Head, London 2011)

Augustine, *Confessions* (Penguin, London 1961)

Julian Baggini, *The Pig That Wants to Be Eaten and 99 Other Thought Experiments* (Granta, London 2006)

Ian G. Barbour, *Religion and Science: Historical and Contemporary Issues* (SCM Press, London 1998)

Robert E. Barron, *The Strangest Way: Walking the Christian Path* (Orbis, New York 2002)

Richard Bauckham, *Bible and Ecology: Rediscovering the Community of Creation* (DLT, London 2010)

Nick Baylis, *The Rough Guide to Happiness* (Rough Guides, London 2009)

Dietrich Bonhoeffer, *Life Together* (SCM Press, London 1992)

Dietrich Bonhoeffer, *The Cost of Discipleship* (SCM Press, London 2001)

Dave Bookless, 'Introduction', in *The Green Bible: A Priceless Message That Doesn't Cost the Earth* (Collins, London 2008)

Dave Bookless, *Planetwise: Dare to Care for God's World* (IVP, Nottingham 2008)

James Brabazon, 'Introduction', in *Albert Schweitzer: Essential Writings* (Orbis, New York 2005)

Ian C. Bradley, *God is Green: Ecology for Christianity and the Environment* (DLT, London 1990)

Kester Brewin, *Other: Loving Self, God and Neighbour in a World of Fractures* (Hodder and Stoughton, London 2010)

Bill Bryson, *A Short History of Nearly Everything* (Black Swan, London 2004)

Martin Buber, *I and Thou* (Continuum, London 2008)

Fritjof Capra, *The Web of Life: A New Synthesis of Mind and Matter* (Flamingo, London 1997)

Denise Carmody and John Carmody, *Serene Compassion* (OUP, Oxford 1996)

Nick Cave, *The Complete Lyrics 1978–2001* (Penguin, London 2001)

Pierre Teilhard de Chardin, *The Phenomenon of Man* (Collins, London 1959)

Pierre Teilhard de Chardin, *Hymn of the Universe* (Collins, London 1970)

Pierre Teilhard de Chardin, *Heart of Matter* (Collins, London 1978)

Pierre Teilhard de Chardin, *Pierre Teilhard de Chardin: Essential Writings* (Orbis, New York 2010)

Paula Clifford, *Angels with Trumpets: The Church in a Time of Global Warming* (DLT, London 2009)

Paul M. Collins, *The Trinity: A Guide for the Perplexed* (T&T Clark, London 2008)

Maria de la Cruz and Mary Richard, *Christ's Life in Us: Grade two teacher's guide: Based on the Kerygmatic approach to Christian doctrine* (Fallons, Dublin 1968)

Roald Dahl, *Fantastic Mr Fox* (Penguin, London 2007)

Richard Dawkins, *The Selfish Gene* (OUP, Oxford 2006)

Richard Dawkins, *The God Delusion* (Black Swan, London 2007)

Cecilia Deane-Drummond, *Eco-Theology* (DLT, London 2008)

Calvin B. DeWitt, 'Reading the Bible through a Green Lens', in *The Green Bible: A Priceless Message That Doesn't Cost the Earth* (Collins, London 2008)

Annie Dillard, *Pilgrim at Tinker Creek* (Harper Perennial, New York 2007)

Ben Dupre, *50 Philosophy Ideas You Really Need to Know* (Quercus, London 2007)

Henry Van Dyke, *The Other Wise Man* (Public Domain Books, Kindle edition 2004)

Mary C. Earle, *Celtic Christian Spirituality* (SPCK, London 2012)

William Eckhardt, *Compassion: Toward a Science of Value* (CPRI, Ontario 1972)

Stefan Einhorn, *The Art of Being Kind* (Sphere, London 2008)

T. S. Eliot, 'The Journey of the Magi', in T. S. Eliot, *Collected Poems 1909–62* (Faber and Faber, London 2002)

Robert Ellsberg, 'Introduction', in *Charles de Foucauld: Essential Writings* (Orbis, New York 1999)

Maggie Fergusson, *War Child to War Horse* (Fourth Estate, London 2012)

E. M. Forster, *A Passage to India* (Penguin, London 2005)

Richard J. Foster and James Bryan Smith (eds), *Devotional Classics: Selected Readings for Individuals and Groups* (Hodder and Stoughton, London 2003)

Charles de Foucauld, *Charles de Foucauld: Essential Writings* (Orbis, New York 1999)

Matthew Fox, *The Coming of the Cosmic Christ: The Healing of Mother Earth and the Birth of a Global Renaissance* (HarperOne, New York 1988)

Matthew Fox, *A Spirituality Named Compassion and the Healing of the Global Village, Humpty Dumpty and Us* (Harper & Row, New York 1990)

Viktor E. Frankl, *Man's Search for Meaning: The Classic Tribute to Hope from the Holocaust* (Rider, London 2004)

Sue Gerhardt, *The Selfish Society: How We All Forgot to Love One Another and Made Money Instead* (Simon & Schuster, London 2010)

Paul Gilbert, *The Compassionate Mind: A New Approach to Life's Challenges* (Constable, London 2010)

Victoria Glendinning, *Leonard Woolf: A Biography* (Free, New York 2006)

Dorothy Frances Gurney, 'God's Garden', in *Poems* (BiblioBazaar, Charleston 2009)

Dafydd ap Gwilym, 'Offeren y Llwyn', in *Poems* (Gomer, Llandysul 1982)

Hildegard of Bingen, *Selected Writings* (Penguin, London 2001)

Etty Hillesum, *Etty Hillesum: Essential Writings* (Orbis, New York 2009)

Thomas Hobbes, *Leviathan* (OUP, Oxford 2008)

Martin J. Hodson and Margot Hodson, *Cherishing the Earth: How to Care for God's Creation* (Monarch, Oxford 2008)

Malcolm Hollick, *The Science of Oneness: A Worldview for the Twenty-First Century* (O, Winchester 2006)

Richard Holloway, *Between the Monster and the Saint* (Canongate, Edinburgh 2008)

Joyce Hollyday, 'Introduction', in *Clarence Jordan: Essential Writings* (Orbis, New York 2003)

Trystan Owain Hughes, *Winds of Change: The Roman Catholic Church and Society in Wales 1916–62* (UWP, Cardiff 2000)

Trystan Owain Hughes, *Finding Hope and Meaning in Suffering* (SPCK, London 2010)

Anne Hunt, *Trinity: Nexus of the Mysteries of Christian Faith* (Orbis, New York 2005)

Lewis Hyde, *The Gift: How the Creative Spirit Transforms the World* (Canongate, Edinburgh 2007)

Kazuo Ishiguro, *Never Let Me Go* (Faber and Faber, London 2006)

Clarence Jordan, *Clarence Jordan: Essential Writings* (Orbis, New York 2003)

Julian of Norwich, *Revelations of Divine Love* (D. S. Brewer, Cambridge, 1998)

Julian of Norwich, *The Showings of Julian of Norwich*, ed. Denise Baker (W. W. Norton, New York, 2005)

Annemarie S. Kidder, 'Introduction', in *Etty Hillesum: Essential Writings* (Orbis, New York 2009)

Martin Luther King Jr, *I Have a Dream: Writings and Speeches that Changed the World* (HarperCollins, San Francisco 1992)

Ursula King, 'Introduction', in *Pierre Teilhard de Chardin: Essential Writings* (Orbis, New York 2010)

Jon Krakauer, *Into the Wild* (Anchor, New York 1997)

Sandra Lacey and Steve Stickley, *People Like Us* (Zondervan, Grand Rapids 2011)

Richard Layard, *Happiness: Lessons from a New Science* (Penguin, London 2006)

C. S. Lewis, *They Stand Together: The Letters of C. S. Lewis to Arthur Greeves* (Collins, London 1979)

C. S. Lewis, *Surprised by Joy* (Fount, London 1998)

C. S. Lewis, *Miracles* (Fount, London 2002)

C. S. Lewis, *Screwtape Letters* (HarperCollins, San Francisco 2002)

Carter Lindberg, *Love: A Brief History through Western Christianity* (Blackwell, Oxford 2008)

James Lovelock, *The Revenge of Gaia: Why the Earth is Fighting Back – and How We Can Still Save Humanity* (Penguin, London 2007)

Robert MacFarlane, *The Wild Places* (Granta, London 2007)

Alaster McGrath, *Science and Religion: An Introduction* (Blackwell, Oxford 1999)

Alister McGrath, *Christian Theology: An Introduction* (Blackwell, Oxford 2001)

Alister McGrath (with Joanna Collicutt McGrath), *The Dawkins Delusion? Atheist Fundamentalism and the Denial of the Divine* (SPCK, London 2007)

Alastair McIntosh, *Rekindling Community: Connecting People, Environment and Spirituality* (Green, Totnes 2008)

Brennan Manning, *The Ragamuffin Gospel* (Authentic, Milton Keynes 2009)

Paul Martin, *Making Happy People: The Nature of Happiness and its Origins in Childhood* (Harper Perennial, London 2006)

Alexander Masters, *Stuart: A Life Backwards* (Harper Perennial, London 2006)

Michael Mayne, *The Enduring Melody* (DLT, London 2007)

Mechthild of Magdeburg, *Flowing Light of the Godhead* (Paulist, New York 1999)

Anthony De Mello, *Awareness* (Zondervan, Grand Rapids 1997)

Thomas Merton, *Contemplative Prayer* (DLT, London 1981)

Thomas Merton, *Thomas Merton: Essential Writings* (Orbis, New York 2000)

C. Robert Mesle, *Process Theology: A Basic Introduction* (Chalice, St Louis 1993)

E. L. Miller and Stanley Grenz, *Introduction to Contemporary Theologies* (Fortress, Minneapolis 1998)

Jürgen Moltmann, *Theology of Hope* (SCM Press, London 2002)

Elisabeth Moltmann-Wendel, *I am My Body: A Theology of Embodiment* (Continuum, London 1995)

Michael Morpurgo, *War Horse* (Egmont, London 2006)

Edwin Muir, 'The Incarnate One', in *Collected Poems* (Faber and Faber, London 1984)

Daniel Nettle, *Happiness: The Science Behind Your Smile* (OUP, Oxford 2006)

Henri Nouwen, *The Wounded Healer: Ministry in Contemporary Society* (DLT, London 1994)

Henri Nouwen, Donald P. McNeill and Douglas A. Morrison, *Compassion: A Reflection on the Christian Life* (DLT, London 2008)

Rebecca Nye, *Children's Spirituality: What is it and Why it Matters* (Church House Publishing, London 2009)

Flannery O'Connor, *The Violent Bear It Away: A Novel* (Farrar, Straus and Giroux, New York 2007)

Dianne L. Oliver, 'Introduction', in *Dorothee Soelle: Essential Writings* (Orbis, New York 2006)

Raj Patel, *Stuffed and Starved: From Farm to Fork, the Hidden Battle for the World Food System* (Portobello, London 2008)

John Polkinghorne, *The Faith of a Physicist* (Augsburg Fortress, Minneapolis 1996)

Philip Pullman, *The Good Man Jesus and the Scoundrel Christ* (Canongate, Edinburgh 2010)

Brendan Purcell, *From Big Bang to Big Mystery: Human Origins in the Light of Creation and Evolution* (Veritas, Dublin 2011)

Murray A. Rae and Graham Redding (eds), *More Than a Single Issue* (ATF, Hindmarsh 2002)

Richard Rees, *Simone Weil: A Sketch for a Portrait* (OUP, Oxford 1966)

Lewis Regenstein, *Replenish the Earth: A History of Organized Religions' Treatment of Animals and Nature* (SCM Press, London 1991)

Adrienne Rich, 'Stepping Backward', in *The Fact of a Doorframe: Poems 1950–2001* (W. W. Norton, London 2003)

Matt Ridley, *The Origins of Virtue* (Penguin, London 1997)

Ronald Rolheiser, *Seeking Spirituality: Guidelines for Christian Spirituality for the Twenty-First Century* (Hodder and Stoughton, London 1998)

Jon Ronson, *The Men Who Stare at Goats* (Picador, London 2012)

Thomas Ryan (ed.), *Reclaiming the Body in Christian Spirituality* (Paulist, New York 2004)

Tony Sargent, *Animal Rights and Wrongs: A Biblical Perspective* (Hodder and Stoughton, London 1996)

E. F. Schumacher, *A Guide for the Perplexed* (Vintage, London 1995)

E. F. Schumacher, *Small is Beautiful: A Study of Economics as if People Mattered* (Vintage, London 2011)

Albert Schweitzer, *My Life and Thought* (Unwin, London 1966)

Albert Schweitzer, *The Philosophy of Civilisation* (Prometheus, New York 1987)

Albert Schweitzer, *Albert Schweitzer: Essential Writings* (Orbis, New York 2005)

Brian Selznick, *The Invention of Hugo Cabret* (Scholastic, New York 2007)

Steven Shakespeare and Hugh Rayment-Pickard, *The Inclusive God: Reclaiming Theology for an Inclusive Church* (Canterbury Press, London 2006)

Megan Shore, *Religion and Conflict Resolution: Christianity and South Africa's Truth and Reconciliation Commission* (Ashgate, Farnham 2009)

Dorothee Soelle, *Suffering* (DLT, London 1975)

Dorothee Soelle, *The Strength of the Weak: Toward a Christian Feminist Identity* (Westminster, Philadelphia 1984)

Dorothee Soelle, *Theology for Sceptics: Reflections on God* (Fortress, Minneapolis 1995)

Dorothee Soelle, *The Silent Cry: Mysticism and Resistance* (Fortress, Minneapolis 2001)

Dorothee Soelle, *Choosing Life* (Wipf & Stock, Eugene 2003)

Dorothee Soelle, *Dorothee Soelle: Essential Writings* (Orbis, New York 2006)

Annika Spalde, *A Heart on Fire: Living As a Mystic in Today's World* (Wild Goose, Glasgow 2010)

Peter Stanford, 'Myra: The Paper Devil', in *The Tablet* 23 November 2002

Harriet Beecher Stowe, *Uncle Tom's Cabin: Or, Life Among the Lowly* (Penguin, London 1986)

Henry Suso, *The Life of the Servant* (James Clarke, Cambridge 1982)

Barbara Brown Taylor, 'The Dominion of Love', in *The Green Bible: A Priceless Message That Doesn't Cost the Earth* (Collins, London 2008)

Thich Nhat Hanh, 'Please Call Me by My True Names', in *Peace is Every Step* (Rider, London 1995)

R. S. Thomas, 'Cynddylan on a Tractor', in *Collected Poems 1945–1990* (Phoenix, London 2004)

J. Milburn Thompson, *Justice and Peace: A Christian Primer* (Orbis, New York 2003)

Henry David Thoreau, *Walden; or Life in the Woods* (Dover, New York 1995)

Paul Tournier, *The Person Reborn* (SCM Press, 1972)

Desmond Tutu, *No Future without Forgiveness: A Personal Overview of South Africa's Truth and Reconciliation Commission* (Rider, London 1999)

Desmond Tutu, *God Has a Dream: A Vision of Hope for Our Time* (Rider, London 2004)

Desmond Tutu, *God Is Not a Christian: Speaking Truth in Times of Crisis* (Rider, London 2011)

Ruth Valerio, *'L' is for Lifestyle: Christian Living that doesn't Cost the Earth* (IVP, Nottingham 2008)

Eldin Villafane, *Beyond Cheap Grace: Call for Radical Discipleship, Incarnation, and Justice* (Eerdmans, Grand Rapids 2006)

Alice Walker, *The Color Purple* (Phoenix, London 2004)

Simone Weil, *Simone Weil: Essential Writings* (Orbis, New York 1998)

Simone Weil, *Gravity and Grace* (Routledge, London 2002)

Lynn White Jr, 'The Historical Roots of Our Ecologic Crisis', in *Science*, 10 March 1967

Walt Whitman, 'There Was a Child Went Forth Every Day', in *The Complete Poems of Walt Whitman* (Wordsworth, Ware 2006)

Richard Wilkinson and Kate Pickett, *The Spirit Level: Why Equality is Better for Everyone* (Penguin, London 2010)

Jane Williams, *The Fellowship of the Three: Exploring the Trinity* (Canterbury Press, London 2006)

Barbara Wood, *Our World, God's World: Readings, Reflections and Prayers on the Environment* (BRS, Oxford 1992)

N. T. Wright, 'Jesus is Coming – Plant a Tree', in *The Green Bible: A Priceless Message That Doesn't Cost the Earth* (Collins, London 2008)

Philip Yancey, *What's so Amazing about Grace?* (Zondervan, Grand Rapids 2002)

Philip Yancey, *Rumours of Another World: What on Earth Are We Missing?* (Zondervan, Grand Rapids 2004)

William P. Young, *The Shack* (Hodder and Stoughton, London 2008)

Wolfram Von Eschenbach, *Parzival* (Penguin, London 1980)